DUBAI
REALTY
CHECK

AR. JASMINE ARORA

PASSIONPRENEUR®
PUBLISHING

AR. JASMINE ARORA

DUBAI
REALTY
CHECK

NAVIGATING REAL ESTATE **NIGHTMARES**

DO NOT BUY REAL ESTATE BEFORE READING THIS!

PASSIONPRENEUR®
PUBLISHING

Print: 978-1-76124-186-4
E-book: 978-1-76124-188-8
Hardback: 978-1-76124-187-1

Publishing information
Publishing and design facilitated by Passionpreneur Publishing
A division of Passionpreneur Organization Pty Ltd
ABN: 48640637529

Melbourne, VIC | Australia
www.passionpreneurpublishing.com

Dubai Realty Check is dedicated
to all first-time buyers, investors,
mortgage buyers, sellers and property advisors
who are committed to making wise decisions.
I am confident that by the end of this book,
you will say, 'I'm proud to have foresight
instead of hindsight—and of avoiding
the "I wish I knew" feeling.'

Figure 1. Skyline of Dubai from the sea, 2024

"Time is on your side to produce and prosper so don't stop until you seize the opportunity."*

—HIS HIGHNESS SHEIKH MOHAMMED BIN RASHID AL MAKTOUM

---

*   https://sheikhmohammed.ae/en-us/quotes

Figure 2. The author driving towards Burj Khalifa, 2023

TABLE OF CONTENTS

ACKNOWLEDGEMENTS

Embarking on this journey of exploring the pitfalls and triumphs within the Dubai real estate market has been a collective effort, and I am profoundly grateful to all who played a role in shaping this book.

To the individuals who graciously shared their real-time experiences concerning the challenges of investing, buying, mortgaging and selling in the Dubai real estate landscape—your stories were the beating heart of our research. Your resilience and openness inspired me to delve deeper, and for that, I extend heartfelt thanks.

To His Highness Sheikh Mohammed bin Rashid Al Maktoum, we express our deepest gratitude for your visionary leadership and the abundant opportunities Dubai has provided to residents and investors alike. Your unwavering commitment to excellence has shaped a city that stands as a beacon of progress and innovation.

To my dear late grandpa, my grandma, my parents, my brother Sidak and the entire Arora family, whose unwavering love, support and commitment to my education laid the foundation for my endeavours, I express my deepest gratitude. Special thanks to my bestie Claudine, my friends Laxmi, Chandan bhai, Jenny, Sanam, Rabia, and Rakesh, my colleagues, and my mentors (Mohamed Magdy, Ryan Serhant, Tom Ferry, Ben Bandari, Tammana, Jai bhai, Hitin bhai, Sam Ayache, Dan Martel and many more). Thank you for being the pillars that supported me through the twists and turns of my life and career. Thanks to my loyal clients (aka friends), who not only trust my advice and service in real estate but also entrust me with their properties completely.

Thanks to Anthony Joseph, who connected me with Moustafa Hamwi, CEO of Passionpreneur Publishing. And a thank you to his team for helping me to edit and publish my book.

A nod to the vast universe, from which all things emanate, for guiding my path and providing the opportunities that led to the creation of this work.

Last but certainly not least, I extend my sincere thanks to you, dear reader. Your engagement with my experiences and insights is what breathes life into these pages. **As I invite you to share your own stories and nightmares in Dubai real estate, I look forward to building a community of shared wisdom.** Your feedback will not only shape future editions but will also contribute to the collective knowledge of those navigating the complex world of real estate.

Thank you all for being an integral part of this journey.

Warm regards,
Jasmine

AUTHOR'S NOTE

All of the included stories are inspired by real events but have been fictionalized, and any resemblance to actual persons is coincidental. It is important to clarify that neither Property Monitor nor any developer has compensated me for promotion. I'm simply sharing my genuine advice, knowledge, opinions and experiences. (Perhaps they should consider paying me for the glowing reviews, though.)

In the ever-evolving landscape of Dubai laws, the content presented in this book reflects the state of affairs up to Q2 2024. Through narratives, analysis and advice, we aim to provide insights that resonate with the legal environment of Dubai before and up to this period. Please be mindful that laws and regulations may continue to evolve beyond this timeframe.

Figure 3. The author on Kite Beach, Dubai, 2023

INTRODUCTION

As I dipped my toes into the crystal-clear waters of Kite Beach, with the iconic, towering Burj Khalifa on my right and the majestic Burj Al Arab gleaming on my left, I felt the Dubai breeze whisper secrets of opportunity and danger. Little did I realise that amid the glitz and glamour of this city of dreams lurked the wild, untamed terrain of its real estate jungle, where fortunes rise and fall like sandcastles at high tide. Are you overwhelmed by the Dubai real estate jungle, too?

Are you fascinated by the opulent world of Dubai—a city that sparkles with architectural splendour, where fortunes are forged and opportunities abound?

BEWARE!

It is also a dynamic arena where towering skyscrapers mirror the highs and lows of the financial world. In this book, we delve into the heart of this dynamic landscape, not just as passive observers but also as active participants.

This is not your typical property guide—it's a riveting exploration into the gripping real-time experiences of first-time buyers, seasoned investors, mortgage enthusiasts and daring real estate warriors conquering the Dubai market. The goal of this book isn't just to tell stories. I want to arm you with the 'know-how' from real-life experiences, so you can stay savvy as you navigate Dubai's real estate maze.

Picture Adam, lured by the promise of a swanky villa, dancing into the fray with the ambitious Lata and the slick agent Robert. But wait, hold your breath! Behind the glitz and glam lurked a hefty bill of AED2.2 million in overdue fees. Adam's rollercoaster ride is just a taste of the surprises awaiting you on these pages. We'll delve into his escapade later—but for now, let's just say it's a wild ride!

Within these pages, you will find market analyses and advice from seasoned real estate experts. With the right knowledge, you'll become not just an investor but a *conqueror*.

Brace yourself for a rollercoaster ride through the highs of success and the lows of property nightmares. We will be dissecting real-time stories that echo the pulse of the Dubai real estate jungle. It's not just about understanding—it's about seizing the potential that Dubai offers.

First, a cautionary word. 'Beware, those who have been burnt by the fire: They often have fiery tales to share.'

This is not just a book; it's your insider's guide to Dubai's real estate goldmine. It's about learning from real-life experiences to safeguard your investments and make the most of the lucrative opportunities Dubai has to offer. So, are you ready to embark on this real estate odyssey?

This book will not tell you how to beat the market, but it *will* show you:

1. Strategies you can employ to reduce the risk of enduring permanent losses in Dubai real estate investment.
2. Approaches you can adopt to enhance the probability of securing your home in Dubai with a smooth transaction.
3. How to steer clear of the often-overlooked pitfalls in Dubai's real estate market.

The Vision

Most importantly, the vision of this book is to create a community where we all are connected on this journey.

P.S. We've got a little surprise for you at the end.

Happy reading!
Jasmine Arora

"I once read an article in a foreign newspaper saying: luck smiles back at Dubai. I respond: when they want to diminish your achievements, they attribute them to luck."

—HIS HIGHNESS SHEIKH MOHAMMED BIN RASHID AL MAKTOUM, VICE PRESIDENT AND PRIME MINISTER OF THE UAE AND RULER OF DUBAI

CHAPTER **1**

THE DUBAI THAT SHAPED ME

In the heart of Dubai, amid the golden sands and azure waters, lies a tale as captivating as the landscape itself. It is a tale that I, Jasmine, have the honour of sharing with you.

Let's take it from the beginning, my friend.

Finding My Own Home

So, there I was, diving headfirst into the wild world of property hunting. Armed with nothing but my architectural vision, optimism and a Dubizzle account, I set out to find my dream home.

My first stop was Agent #1. But guess what? They must have mistaken *appointment* for *suggestion* because they waltzed in a cool 40 minutes late. I half-expected a red carpet rollout!

Next up was Agent #2. They had a knack for surprises, all right. The property they showed me? Let's just say it looked like the 'before' picture in a home renovation show—I'm talking about major fixer-upper vibes!

Undeterred, I soldiered on to Agent #3. Parking was supposed to be their ace in the hole, but it turned out to be more of a parking lot myth than a reality. I guess *spacious parking* means something else in their dictionary!

After enduring more plot twists than *Star Wars*, I stumbled upon my real estate fairy godmother, Heena. She didn't just find me a home, she found me *the* home—a cosy little sanctuary that felt like it had been plucked straight from my dreams.

And that's when it hit me: Amid all the chaos and craziness, there's a diamond in the rough. Inspired by Heena's stellar service (and maybe fuelled by a tad too much *Karak Chai*), I vowed to shake up the real estate game … because who says house hunting can't be a comedy of errors?

That wasn't all; it wasn't until a chance encounter that I truly understood the depth of my calling.

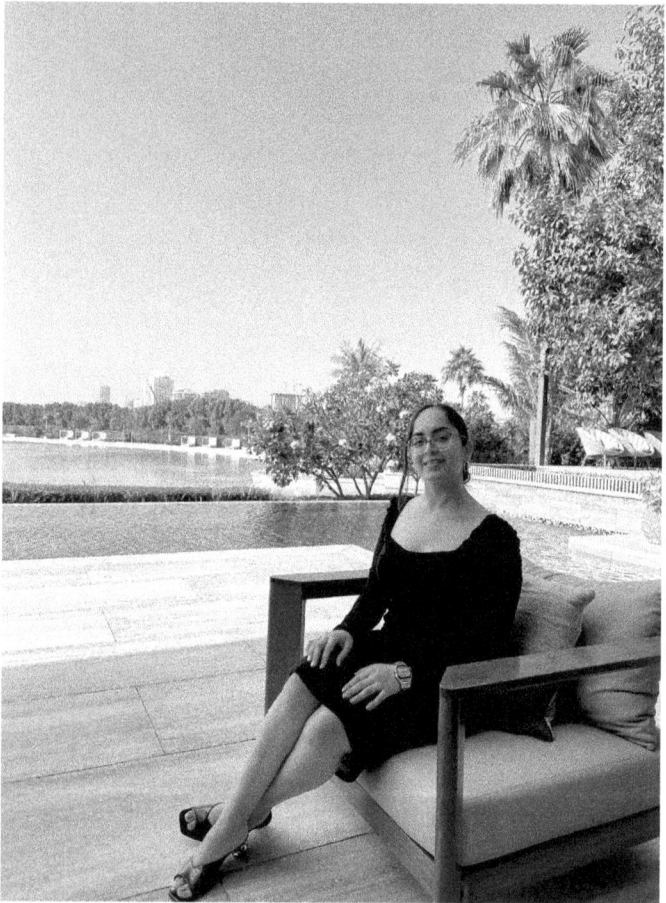

Figure 4. The author in Tilal Al Ghaf, 2023

A Pregnant Lady Changed My Life

A charming pregnant lady, her eyes filled with desperation and hope, was standing amid the quiet on the beach in Tilal Al Ghaf. She was on the verge of surrender, ready to abandon her quest for a place to call home, until fate intervened most unexpectedly.

On a crisp summer morning, our paths crossed. As she poured her heart out, recounting the trials and tribulations of her search for a home, I couldn't help but be drawn into the depths of her despair. Her tale resonated with me in a way I couldn't quite explain, stirring something deep within my soul.

Together, we embarked on a journey of discovery with determination and resolve.

A Moment of Truth: Recalling my Grandma's Wisdom

It was then that I recalled the words of my sweet grandma: 'You can either put your hand in the fire to realise it's hot, or learn from other people's experiences who got burnt and avoid that.' Her words echoed in my mind, guiding me like a compass through the tangled web of uncertainty surrounding us.

It was from these shared experiences that I felt called to action, driven by a deep desire to make a difference in the lives of others. Thus, the idea of compiling a collection of real estate nightmare stories was born—not to instil fear or doubt but to shine a light on the human side of the real estate journey.

I have encountered my fair share of real estate horror stories—tales of dreams turned sour, deals gone wrong and nightmares that haunt buyers and sellers alike. But instead of turning away from these stories, I leaned in, listened and learned.

Through years of immersion in the industry as a COA-certified architect and Real Estate Regulatory Agency (RERA)–certified real estate advisor, I have witnessed firsthand the pitfalls and traps that can ensnare even the most cautious buyers and sellers. I have seen everything from hidden fees and dishonest agents to legal disputes and property nightmares. But with each tale of woe, I have gained invaluable insights into what went wrong and, more importantly, how it could have been avoided.

As an architect-turned-property advisor specialising in selling homes in Tilal Al Ghaf and many villa communities, I have had the privilege of witnessing the ebb and flow of countless real estate journeys—each one a unique blend of hopes, dreams and challenges. All these experiences have eventually helped me arrange smooth transactions for multiple investors and homeowners in Dubai.

Figure 5. Author in front of Aura twin villa in Tilal Al Ghaf, 2023

I want to offer you a guiding hand through the pages of this book, even if we have never met. By sharing the stories of struggles, triumphs and hard-learned lessons, my aim is to help you navigate the real estate landscape with confidence and ease.

So, whether you're a first-time buyer, an investor, or a seasoned homeowner, my book shares real-life experiences of property investors and families who overcame challenges and built trust in Dubai's dynamic property market. By providing clear guidance, understanding of the processes, and continued support, my book will empower you to make informed decisions, ensuring you have the right tools and ethical approach to succeed in this vibrant and growing market.

This book is your roadmap to smooth transactions and successful outcomes. It is a testament to the power of learning from others' experiences so you can avoid the pitfalls and make informed decisions on your own real estate journey. Let's embark on this adventure together, and may it lead you to your dream home with grace and certainty.

The Silver Lining

If you're ready to learn from the mistakes of others and avoid the pitfalls that can turn your real estate dreams into nightmares, then come with me. Together, we'll uncover the hidden dangers lurking in the shadows and emerge stronger, wiser and better prepared to navigate the world of real estate. Welcome to the journey of learning from others' experiences.

I am keen to hear your experiences and happy to help you with your journey personally.

"Only a fool learns from his own mistakes. The wise man learns from the mistakes of others."

—OTTO VON BISMARCK

CHAPTER 2

LIFE LESSONS FROM
THE PROPERTY MARKET

Ever heard the saying, 'Learn from the mistakes of others?'

In the world of real estate, these mistakes can be costly. But what if I told you that the keys to your success lie within these cautionary tales?

This book is a comprehensive guide that sheds light on the real estate nightmares faced by investors, first-time homebuyers, mortgage seekers and sellers alike.

Through real-life based stories and expert analysis, this book aims to equip you with the knowledge and insights to navigate the Dubai real estate market with confidence and caution.

While Dubai's real estate market presents exciting and lucrative opportunities, it's essential to navigate it carefully to ensure a smooth transaction. By staying informed and prepared, buyers, sellers, and investors can easily avoid common challenges like unexpected fees, paperwork complexities, and other potential obstacles, allowing them to make the most of their real estate ventures.

Real-life Based Stories

By sharing stories based on real experiences, this book seeks to expose these misconceptions and empower readers to make informed decisions. Rather than viewing real estate nightmares as setbacks, we can see them as valuable learning opportunities.

Each story shared in this book serves as a cautionary tale, highlighting common pitfalls and offering practical advice on how to avoid them. By adopting a proactive and informed approach, readers can safeguard their investments and navigate the Dubai real estate market with confidence.

Generally, learning from the experiences of others is one of the most effective ways to avoid repeating common mistakes. Through in-depth analysis and expert commentary, this book provides readers with the tools and insights they need to make smarter decisions and protect their interests in the Dubai real estate market.

This book is divided into four sections.

First-time Buyers: Picture this. You, a wide-eyed dreamer, are ready to stake your claim in Dubai's dazzling skyline—but hold on tight, because hidden costs, financing fiascos and property disputes are lurking around every corner. It's like navigating a maze with a blindfold and a map drawn by a toddler. Will you emerge unscathed, or will your dreams of homeownership be dashed faster than you can say 'golden visa?'

Mortgage Buyers: Ah, the joys of mortgage shopping in Dubai! It's like speed dating, but instead of finding your soulmate, you're trying to avoid predatory lenders and foreclosure faster than you can say 'variable interest rate'. Will you find your dream home or end up drowning in a sea of paperwork and regret? Only time will tell!

Investors: Think you've got what it takes to conquer the Dubai real estate market? Think again! Dive into the tales of investors who thought they were playing Monopoly but ended up in a game of Jumanji. From unexpected legal hurdles to deals gone sour faster than week-old hummus, these stories will have you clutching your wallet tighter than a camel clings to its last drop of water.

Sellers: Calling all would-be sellers! Get ready for a whirlwind adventure through the ups and downs of offloading your property in Dubai. From lowball offers to delays longer than the line at a brunch buffet, selling your slice of paradise has never been more thrilling (or exasperating). Will you emerge victorious or end up crying into your palm frond–shaped cocktail? Grab your sunscreen and find out!

Join us on this zany journey through Dubai's real estate circus, where the only thing crazier than the market is the cast of characters trying to navigate it. With laughter, tears and maybe a few palm trees thrown in for good measure, it's sure to be a ride you won't soon forget!

Welcome to the wild world of Dubai real estate, where the sands of opportunity shift beneath your feet faster than you can say 'escrow account'. Strap in for a rollercoaster ride through the highs and lows of property ownership, where the only thing more unpredictable than the market itself is your neighbour's taste in lawn decorations. Let's begin!

Let's embark on a journey through stories that resonate with both vulnerability and resilience. Through trials, we peel back the layers of Dubai's real estate landscape, discovering lessons that shimmer with both caution and hope. Let's learn from their courage and unearth the wisdom they have gained, for in their narratives lie not only cautionary tales but also testaments to the enduring strength of Dubai's real estate market, guided by a government committed to ensuring the safety and prosperity of its investors.

PART I

FIRST-TIME
BUYERS

What would you do if your perfect property turned into a legal night-mare? Join Shankaran Pillai's journey to ponder: Would you forge ahead ... or hit the brakes?

CHAPTER 3

FROM DREAM VILLA TO LEGAL QUANDARIES:

Shankaran Pillai's Dubai Real Estate
Safari Unleashes the Unexpected!

Picture this: Shankaran, a savvy entrepreneur with an eye for a killer property, stumbles upon the villa of his dreams. The furnishings? Impeccable. The layout? A masterpiece. The community vibe? Family-oriented heaven. The property was still under construction, owned by an individual and linked to a transferable payment plan with the developer, which meant easy and flexible payments for Shankaran.

Now, you would think this is a match made in real estate heaven, right? Well, hold your horses. Shankaran, being the go-getter he is, wants to seal the deal under his company name. Cue the bureaucratic hurdle—the notorious No Objection Certificate (NOC) from the licensing authority. But does Shankaran back down? No way! He dives into the paperwork tango, aiming to hustle that NOC in just a couple of days.

But here's where the plot thickens. Despite the NOC hustle, Shankaran's agent, sensing an opportunity, pushes him to kick off the deal prematurely. A 10% security deposit flies from Shankaran's hands, and a manual Memorandum of Understanding (MOU/Contract F) is born. Terms, conditions and a dash of optimism—all in one document.

Fast-forward, and Shankaran is on the hunt for those juicy details about the seller's dues to the developer. Suddenly, his once-talkative agent goes silent. Red flag, anyone?

Undeterred, Shankaran pings the seller directly, only to discover a synchronised silence.

Smelling something fishy, Shankaran taps into his inner Sherlock and consults a legal maestro. The verdict? This deal is as legal as a three-dollar bill. No Dubai land system stroll, no Form A and *certainly* no Form F (manual MOUs are not valid anymore in Dubai). Shankaran finds himself in a sticky situation, with his security deposit playing hide-and-seek with the elusive agent.

The real estate drama continues, folks. Shankaran is caught in a web of uncertainty, but you better believe he's not backing down.

Market Analysis

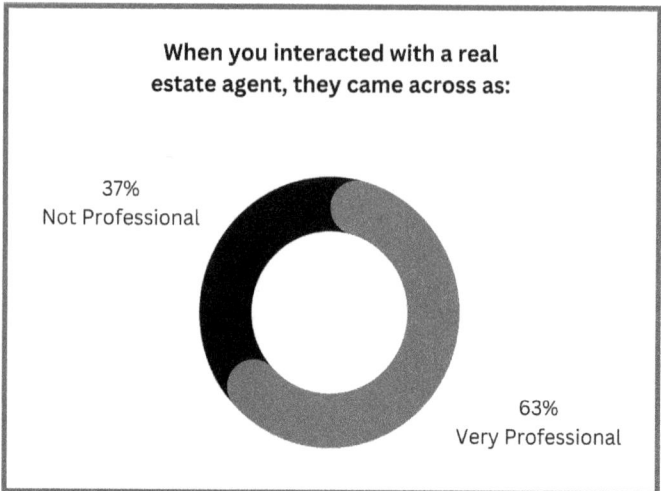

Figure 6. Graph based on Bayut email and social media agents
behaviours survey – September 2018
Source: (Bayut, 2018)

Bayut conducted a survey among property seekers on their platform in 2018, revealing that 63% of users perceived the agents on the portal as professionals. I can confidently say, engaging with property portals such as Bayut significantly improves the probability of encountering professional agents.

For users navigating Property Finder, it is advisable to specifically explore listings curated by super agents. However, even in such instances, it remains crucial to exercise caution. When interacting with agents on these platforms, always prioritise the request for their RERA license to ensure they are registered with RERA. This precautionary step becomes especially relevant in a market where the presence of unregistered agents poses potential risks in property transactions.

To be a savvy buyer, it is important to first do your own due diligence.

1. If a property is too good to be true, it probably is!
2. If you are being pushed into signing or accepting a document that is suspect, get a second opinion.
3. To manage expectations, be open to hearing the negatives and positives.

Conclusion

It is important to understand the system of Dubai's real estate market and its rules and regulations. The final sales contract (MOU/Contract F) is only valid if signed online via the Dubai Land Department website.

Your dream home isn't just a house—it's your hard-earned money on the line. Before you dive into a deal, you have got to do your homework. We're talking due diligence.

Here's the deal. Don't just roll the dice with any random broker. This is your dream we are talking about, not some casual Friday night out. Seek out the heavy hitters—those reputable agents who know the game inside out.

It's like this: You wouldn't pick a random surgeon for a life-changing operation, right? Your dream home deserves the same level of attention. Find an agent who is not just in it for the commission but is genuinely invested in making your dream a reality.

Your money, your dream—they deserve the A-team. So, before you jump into the real estate arena, gear up with the right agents and get savvy about the sales and purchase processes.

PRO TIP !

1. **Manual MOU:** A sales contract aligned with the procedural standards set by the Dubai Land Department is imperative. All contracts are created on the Dubai Land Department website, and you will receive them by email once created. A manual MOU no longer holds value in Dubai real estate.

2. **Caution:** While the temptation of expediting a deal may be enticing, attempting to secure a significant transaction without adhering to established protocols is akin to entering a race without properly lacing up one's sneakers.

Elevate the standard for your dream home, ensuring adherence to established procedures.

Let's learn more from another first-time buyer's dark experience.

"You can fool all the people some of the time, and some of the people all the time, but you cannot fool all the people all the time."

—ABRAHAM LINCOLN

CHAPTER 4

LISTING LIES:

David's Encounter with the
Phantom Mansion of Dubai

David, an aspiring international real estate investor, stumbled upon a captivating online listing for a historic mansion in the heart of Dubai. The property, presented by a reputable real estate agency, boasted rich architectural details, a sprawling garden and a storied past. Eager to make a unique investment, David scheduled a viewing.

Upon arriving at the address, he was puzzled to find a completely different property—a modest house that bore no resemblance to the grand mansion he had seen online. Perplexed, David contacted the real estate agent who had listed the property, only to receive vague explanations and promises to investigate the discrepancy. So, he figured he would drown his sorrows in a Starbucks coffee, hoping the caffeine would do the trick.

Determined to unravel the mystery, David dug deeper into the history of the mansion he saw in the listing. To his surprise, he discovered that the images and details provided were not of the property in question but of a different, more luxurious estate in a different location.

Realising he had fallen victim to a misleading sales listing, David decided to expose the deceptive practices. He shared his experience on social media, warning others about the importance of verifying property details before making any commitments. His story gained traction, prompting both public outrage and increased scrutiny of the transparency of sale listings.

In response to the incident, regulatory bodies implemented stricter guidelines for real estate agencies to ensure accurate representation in online listings. David's ordeal became a cautionary tale, encouraging prospective buyers to conduct thorough research and demand transparency when exploring property listings in Dubai.

Market Analysis

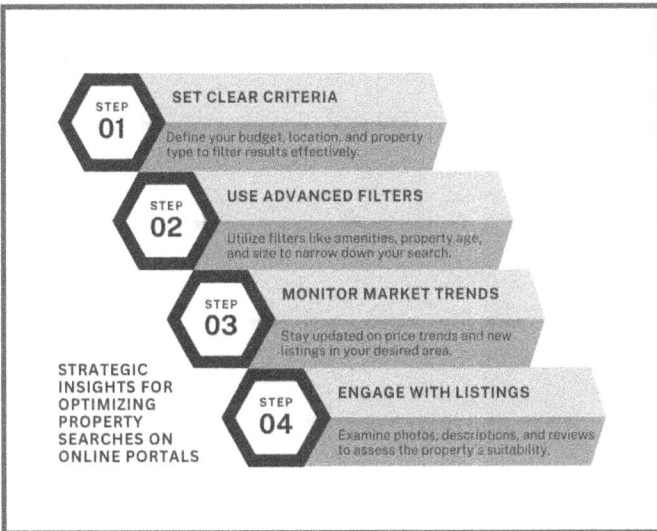

STEP 01 SET CLEAR CRITERIA
Define your budget, location, and property type to filter results effectively.

STEP 02 USE ADVANCED FILTERS
Utilize filters like amenities, property age, and size to narrow down your search.

STEP 03 MONITOR MARKET TRENDS
Stay updated on price trends and new listings in your desired area.

STEP 04 ENGAGE WITH LISTINGS
Examine photos, descriptions, and reviews to assess the property's suitability.

STRATEGIC INSIGHTS FOR OPTIMIZING PROPERTY SEARCHES ON ONLINE PORTALS

Figure 7. Strategic insights for optimizing property searches on online portals

The analysis reveals a strategic approach to optimizing property searches on online portals. By defining your criteria, users can clearly specify their budget, preferred location, and property type for more precise results. Utilizing filters wisely ensures that searches are narrowed down to the most relevant listings. Setting alerts enables users to stay updated with new listings that match their criteria. Thoroughly reviewing listings, including verified ones, provides reliability and accuracy. Engaging with super agents and community experts enhances the process with valuable expertise and local insights. This comprehensive strategy ensures a trustworthy, efficient, and well-informed real estate exploration experience.

Conclusion

In the wild world of online property promotion, there are rules aplenty, but some things slip through the cracks. So, why not play it safe? Stick with verified listings and the super agents you'll find on different portals like Property Finder and Bayut. They've got your back, ensuring what you see is what you get, saving you from any surprises.

PRO TIP !

When it comes to finding your property guide, think of local experts. These folks know their turf like the back of their hand. How to find them? Easy. Check out Instagram, YouTube, Google and of course, Property Finder and Bayut. Let these tools be your treasure map, leading you to the perfect guide who speaks your language and knows just what you need.

There is more to buying and selling in Dubai. Let's look at the tales of investors, some savvy and some not so savvy.

"Impossible is a word used by some people who fear to dream big."*

—HIS HIGHNESS SHEIKH MOHAMMED BIN RASHID AL MAKTOUM

* https://sheikhmohammed.ae/en-us/quotes

CHAPTER 5

TICK TOCK TILAL:

Mohnish's Timely Twist in
Roman's Tale

In this chapter, let's dive into a wild tale of Dubai real estate with Roman, a guy sitting in London, dreaming big after learning about his friend's success in Dubai. So, Roman starts talking to different agents, but there's this one guy, Mohnish, a consistent agent with a knack for following up.

Now, Mohnish pitches this fantastic townhouse in a crystal lagoon community in Tilal Al Ghaf called Elan, originally priced at AED2.3 million. But here's the twist: Mohnish pulls off some magic and snags it for Roman at AED2.05 million!

Sounds like a sweet deal, right?

Figure 8. Elan townhouses in Tilal Al Ghaf, 2024

Thinking it's too much money, Roman gets cold feet and backs out, fearing the market might take a nosedive.

Fast-forward three months, and Mohnish has not given up. He shows Roman how the market is going up; similar properties are now priced at AED2.5 million, but there's an urgent sale at AED2.4 million. Mohnish advises Roman to buy it, but Roman decides to wait until handover, when things might get shaky for some folks who can't pay, and prices may drop. Drama alert!

Handover time comes, and guess what? Mortgage buyers flood the scene, demand shoots through the roof, and supply is like a rare gem. Prices for similar places skyrocket to AED2.8 million. Mohnish gives Roman a nudge and a follow-up, and now Roman is in the regret zone.

But hold your horses! Mohnish, not one to let a story end on a sour note, offers Roman a new chapter—Aura Gardens, an under-construction beauty at AED2.4 million. Roman takes the plunge, and guess what? That property is now worth AED2.7 million! Roman is over the moon, but there's this lingering 'What if?'

Mohnish, being the wise advisor, tells Roman, 'It's never too late to catch a good plot twist in the real estate tale.'

Market Analysis

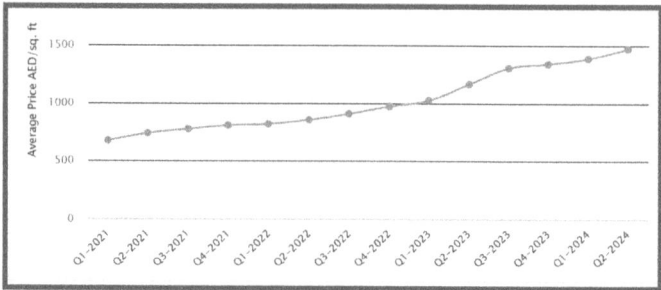

Figure 9. Price Per Square Foot in Elan, Tilal Al Ghaf from 2021 to 2024
Source: (Property Monitor, 2024)

This graph from Property Monitor clearly shows that price per square foot has increased over the years in Tilal Al Ghaf, indicating that investing in communities like Tilal Al Ghaf has always been profitable for investors.

Overall, Dubai's real estate boom is bolstered not only by economic stability and strategic initiatives, but also by progressive policies such as the Golden Visa programme. This initiative allows individuals, including real estate investors, to obtain long-term residency without the need for a local sponsor.

Furthermore, the golden visa extends to entrepreneurs, enabling them to open companies without requiring a local investor in the business. This flexibility has been a game-changer, attracting a wave of investors and business enthusiasts who seek a thriving real estate market and the opportunity to establish and grow businesses within Dubai's vibrant and cosmopolitan landscape.

Waiting may not be the best idea when there's a good deal on offer. Of course, consider the market conditions and location before taking a call.

Conclusion

In the scheme of things, 'Don't wait to buy real estate; buy real estate and wait.' Time is the real hero in this tale.

But here's the plot twist: Location is your sidekick. Choose wisely, and your property becomes a gem. Fumble, and you might be left dreaming of better spots.

So, in the real estate adventure, remember: Act in time, but let location be your map to enduring success.

PRO TIP !

Before diving into an investment in a specific location, examining recent transactions in that area is crucial. This valuable information is readily accessible by the Dubai Government through websites such as Property Monitor, offering insights that can be instrumental in making informed and strategic investment decisions.

Here's another 'buyer beware' tale that would be a great lesson for all of us …

"Real estate cannot be lost or stolen, nor can it be carried away. Purchased with common sense, paid for in full, and managed with reasonable care, it is about the safest investment in the world."

—FRANKLIN D. ROOSEVELT

CHAPTER 6

EVICTION NOTICES AND GENIE WISHES:

Simon's Unconventional Path to
Property Ownership

 What are the things you make sure of when buying a property?

In the hustle and bustle of Dubai's real estate, Simon, a first-time buyer, was caught in the rent hike whirlwind. Tired of watching his hard-earned dirhams vanish into the abyss of increasing rents, he decided to take the plunge and become a property owner.

Simon spotted a property that seemed a promising respite from the rental rollercoaster. The seller, Matt, sent a vacating notice to the tenant from Dubai Courts. Simon was confident and optimistic, swiftly sealing the deal with an MOU—the golden ticket to homeownership.

As the property was transferred into Simon's name, he excitedly signalled his departure to his current landlord. However, the plot took an unexpected turn when he contacted Andrei, the agent. Instead of a smooth transition, Simon encountered a sandstorm of resistance. Andrei, after discussion with current tenant, insisted on a fresh eviction notice, making the process more challenging than anticipated.

Faced with this unexpected twist, Simon turned to the legal counsel for guidance. The verdict? The eviction notice was non-transferable.

Devastated, Simon reluctantly renewed the lease—a pragmatic move which kept his dreams of a new abode on hold for another year, all while bearing the weight of a revised rent decree from his landlord.

Market Analysis

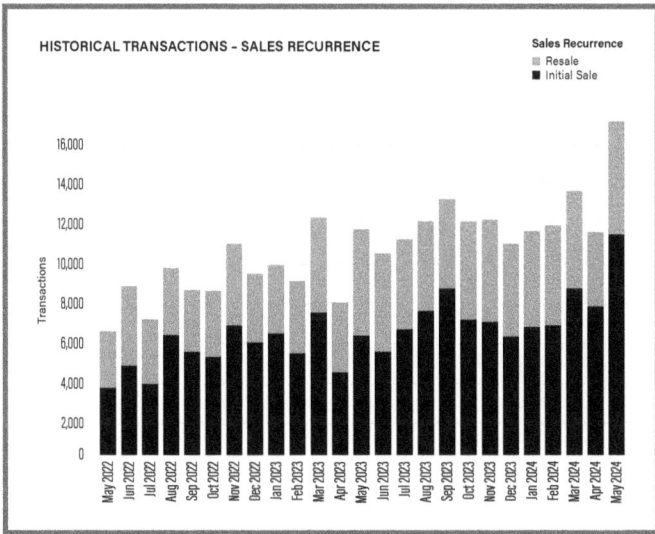

Figure 10. Resale vs Initial Sales 2022–2024
(Property Monitor, 2024)

In May 2024, initial developer sales dominated the market, accounting for a whopping 67% of transactions, a slight dip of 0.5% from the previous month. Meanwhile, resales are gaining traction, now holding 39% of the market according to Property Monitor. This vibrant mix shows a dynamic market where both new and resale properties are thriving.

It's crystal clear from Property Monitor's graph! Initial sales have been leading the charge, especially in 2024. Despite a peak in resale transactions in April 2021, the trend is shifting back towards new developments, which is a goldmine for buyers seeking fresh opportunities.

Conclusion

So, what does this mean for you? If you're like Simon, a first-time buyer ready to dive into Dubai's real estate, this data is your roadmap. Simon's journey, filled with unexpected twists like a non-transferable eviction notice, underscores the importance of staying ahead of market trends and legal intricacies.

In this bustling market, armed with the latest insights, you can confidently navigate your real estate journey. Initial sales are hot right now—don't miss out! Make informed decisions and ride the wave of new opportunities in Dubai's ever-evolving real estate landscape.

PRO TIPS !

1. **Consult Legal Experts:** Seek advice from legal professionals familiar with Dubai's real estate laws to ensure a clear understanding of your rights and obligations.
2. **Verify Notices:** If the property is occupied, validate any eviction notices provided by the seller and confirm their legal standing.
3. **Direct Communication:** Establish direct communication with the current tenant (if applicable) to gauge their intentions and avoid post-purchase surprises.
4. **Consider the Tenant's Perspective:** Understand the tenant's viewpoint and be empathetic in negotiations, aiming for a smooth transition if the property is occupied.
5. **Legal Non-Transferables:** Be aware of legal aspects, such as non-transferable eviction notices, and factor these into your decision-making process.

Let's look at the situation when buyers want to buy with bank financing methods. Whether you are a new or seasoned buyer, Dubai banks provide flexibility to invest in real estate.

Checklist–Before Buying a Property in Dubai

- ☐ Determine your budget.
- ☐ Research the Dubai real estate market.
- ☐ Decide on the type of property you want (apartment, villa, townhouse).
- ☐ Check your eligibility for a mortgage (if applicable).
- ☐ Find a reliable real estate agent.
- ☐ Visit multiple properties to compare options.
- ☐ Verify the property developer's reputation.
- ☐ Understand the legal requirements and paperwork.
- ☐ Negotiate the property price.
- ☐ Review the sales agreement carefully before signing.

**Scan to View
Complete Checklist**

Dare to step into the labyrinth of Dubai's real estate market, where every mortgage holds a tale of its own. Ever wondered what lies beneath the glossy brochures and enticing deals? Join us on an exhilarating journey through the world of mortgage buyers in our next captivating section, where every turn brings forth new challenges and unexpected revelations. Get ready to unravel the mysteries and uncover the lessons hidden within the gripping stories of Sarah, Jaime and others. Are you prepared to venture into the heart of Dubai's real estate nightmares? Let's go!

PART II

MORTGAGE BUYERS

"The journey of a thousand miles begins with one step."

—LAO TZU

CHAPTER 7

THE CANVAS OF CONCEALMENT:

Emily Falls Out of Love

In the heart of Dubai, Emily, an art enthusiast, stumbled upon a quaint villa in an old community that seemed to embody the charm of a hidden oasis. The seller, Olivia, portrayed the property as a masterpiece adorned with strokes of perfection that mirrored Emily's love of aesthetics. Little did she know that beneath the surface, a different narrative unfolded.

Entranced by the picturesque façade, Emily saw the villa as a canvas awaiting her personal touch. Olivia, a convincing storyteller, narrated the tale of an immaculate home embellished with artistic details. Eager to make this her haven, Emily neglected the need for a thorough inspection, relying on the enchanting narrative painted by Olivia.

After the purchase, cracks in the façade began to emerge. *Literal* cracks. What was once a pristine canvas revealed hidden fissures, plumbing issues and structural flaws that eluded Emily's initial gaze. The villa, now hers, resembled less of a masterpiece and more of an unfinished sketch marred by imperfections.

Frustrated by the unforeseen challenges, Emily decided to share her story as a cautionary tale.

She learned that hiring a snagging company before purchasing could have unveiled these concealed issues.

The cracks in the walls, plumbing leaks and structural discrepancies could have been exposed by a diligent inspection.

As Emily navigated the complexities of addressing the undisclosed problems, she became an advocate for prospective buyers, urging them to enlist the expertise of snagging companies before sealing the deal. Her story echoed through the real estate community, emphasising the importance of looking beyond the surface, hiring professionals to scrutinise the details and not being swayed solely by the artistic narrative of sellers.

In the end, Emily transformed her flawed canvas into a true masterpiece, not just in appearance but also as a testament to resilience. In the process, she learned an invaluable lesson: Always hire a snagging company before letting the strokes of deception paint your real estate dreams.

Analysis

Figure 11. riina Café in Tilal Al Ghaf

Picture this: Dubai's real estate scene is buzzing with excitement as brand-new communities are cropping up, courtesy of big developers like EMAAR and Majid Al Futtaim. The city's getting a makeover … and everyone wants a piece of the action.

Now, what sets these new communities apart? Well, besides the shiny new buildings and fancy amenities, they come with a sweet deal called the defect liability period (DLP). Basically, it's like having a warranty for your home—any issues, big or small, get fixed up by the developer for free within the first year. Talk about peace of mind, right?

Take Tilal Al Ghaf, for example. It's the new kid on the block, offering a range of homes from modest AED3 million pads to jaw-dropping AED200 million mansions. Plus, it's got this swanky crystal lagoon that's the talk of the town. Ever heard of the Elysian Mansion? Yep, it's right in Tilal Al Ghaf, adding a touch of luxury to the neighbourhood.

Conclusion

In the tapestry of Dubai's real estate tales, Emily's experience serves as a poignant reminder that beneath the allure of picturesque façades lie hidden realities. As she navigated the pitfalls of her purchase, her journey unfolded as a cautionary tale, urging prospective buyers to look beyond the surface.

Emily's transformation from disillusionment to advocacy highlights the importance of diligence and expertise in navigating the complexities of real estate transactions.

As Dubai's landscape evolves with the emergence of new communities like Tilal Al Ghaf, Elysian Mansion stands as a beacon of promise amid the city's real estate canvas. With a defect liability period offering peace of mind and a range of offerings catering to diverse preferences, these developments symbolise Dubai's commitment to quality and innovation.

In the end, Emily's flawed canvas transformed into a masterpiece of resilience, echoing the sentiment that in Dubai's ever-evolving real estate scene, diligence and discernment are the brushstrokes that paint dreams into reality.

PRO TIP !

The lesson is clear: Hiring a snagging company before sealing the deal could unveil concealed issues lurking beneath a property's charm. (Or buy a house in a brand-new community.)

A snagging company is a professional service provider specialising in inspecting newly constructed properties for defects, faults and deviations from quality standards. Their primary role is identifying any issues with the property's construction or finish, providing comprehensive reports to developers and buyers to facilitate necessary corrections and ensuring the property meets expected quality benchmarks.

Here's why you should consider hiring a snagging company in the real estate market:

1. **Quality Assurance**: A snagging company conducts thorough inspections to identify any defects or issues with the property, ensuring it meets the promised quality standards.
2. **Protecting Investment**: By uncovering potential problems early on, buyers can avoid costly

repairs or disputes after purchasing the property, thus safeguarding their investment.

3. **Negotiation Power**: Armed with a snagging report detailing deficiencies, buyers have stronger leverage for negotiating with developers to address issues or potentially adjust the purchase price.

4. **Peace of Mind**: Hiring a snagging company gives buyers confidence and peace of mind, knowing that their investment is backed by a professional assessment of the property's condition.

5. **Legal Protection**: In case of disputes over the property's condition post-purchase, a snagging report serves as valuable documentation to support the buyer's claims and protect their legal rights.

Overall, hiring a snagging company empowers buyers to make informed decisions, mitigate risks and ensure they invest in a property that meets their expectations of quality and integrity.

"An ounce of prevention is worth a pound of cure."

—BENJAMIN FRANKLIN

CHAPTER 8

MORTGAGE MAYHEM:

Sarah's Journey in Saving AED
and Losing Dreams

In the dazzling city of Dubai, Sarah set her sights on a dream villa, a stunner priced at a hefty AED7 million. Enter Alex, a charming seller juggling mortgages, and Mia, the real estate agent weaving dreams and, of course, the subtle yet crucial mention of conveyancing.

Promising an easy ride through the mortgage maze, Mia wisely suggested getting conveyancing to smooth out the paperwork wrinkles. However, with dreams of saving some dirhams, Sarah and Alex thought they could handle it themselves and decided to skip the suggested conveyancing, missing the chance to avoid a headache later.

But, lo and behold, the promise of simplicity turned into a swirl of hidden fees and jargon as they waded through paperwork. The villa—worth a cool AED7 million—that had once looked like a fairytale home started to cast shadows of doubt.

As the closing date neared, Sarah realised that the limited timeline might lead to losing the 10% security deposit. Adding salt to the wound, the mortgage she secured was only 70% of the villa's value—not the more manageable 80% she expected—because the property value was above AED5 million.

Now stuck in a financial and timeline maze, Sarah found her dream turning into a money pit. The excitement of owning an AED7 million villa in Dubai faded into a frustrating reality check.

Word of Sarah's misadventure spread like wildfire. Her story echoed through the streets and cafés, a cautionary tale in Dubai's buzzing real estate scene. It's a reminder that even in the city of dreams, sharks and dream-weavers are lurking, ready to turn your happily-ever-after home into a mortgage nightmare. And sometimes, a little investment in the required expertise, like conveyancing, can save you a world of trouble, even if it means parting with a bit of cash.

Market Analysis

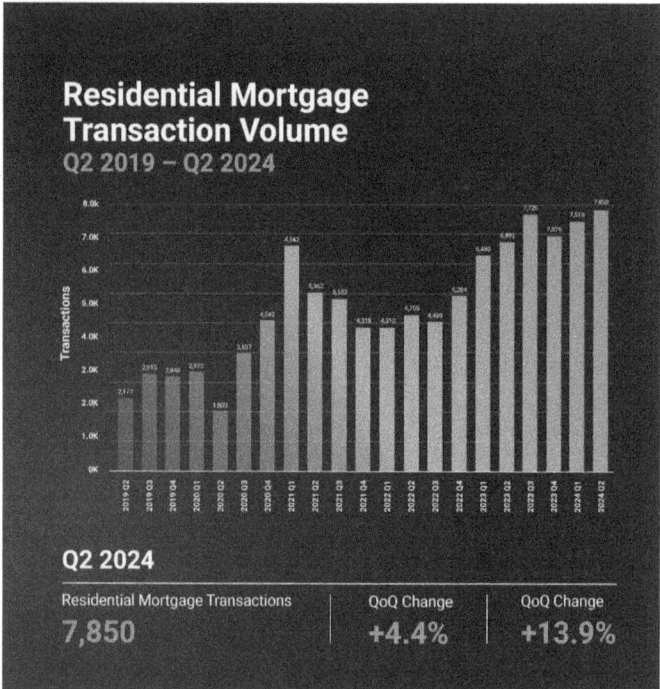

Figure 12. Residential Mortgage Transaction Volume Q2 2019 – Q2 2024
(Property Monitor, 2024)

In Q2 2024, Dubai's real estate market hit a new high with residential mortgage transactions soaring to 7,850—a 13.9% jump from the previous quarter, as highlighted by Property Monitor. This surge reflects a booming interest in property financing, a trend every savvy buyer needs to watch.

Now, imagine Sarah's journey. She eyed a dream villa priced at AED7 million. With the real estate market buzzing, Sarah faced the typical mortgage hurdles. But here's the twist—she and Alex, the seller, skipped the crucial step of conveyancing, thinking they could handle the paperwork maze themselves.

Big mistake! As they drowned in hidden fees and convoluted terms, Sarah's dream home started looking more like a financial trap. The mortgage she secured only covered 70% of the villa's value, leaving her scrambling to cover the shortfall. The fear of losing her 10% security deposit loomed large.

Conclusion

This story isn't just about Sarah; it's a wake-up call for all buyers in this red-hot market. With residential mortgage transactions climbing, it's essential to invest in expert conveyancing. As shown by the latest Property Monitor data, the stakes are high and the market is moving fast. Don't let your dream home turn into a nightmare—get the right help, avoid the pitfalls, and make informed decisions to secure your slice of Dubai's real estate heaven.

PRO TIP !

As investors navigate the mortgage maze, the wisdom of seeking professional guidance becomes paramount, ensuring a smoother journey towards their real estate goals.

In a mortgage transaction, always hire a conveyancer to make your life easier.

From buying to selling, let's now take a look at the other side of the coin.

"Those who believed that Dubai's economy and success were based solely on the real estate sector were pointedly wrong."*

—HIS HIGHNESS SHEIKH MOHAMMED BIN RASHID AL MAKTOUM

---

* https://sheikhmohammed.ae/en-us/quotes

CHAPTER 9

DESERT DANCE:

Jake's Cha-cha with Dubai
Real Estate

Enter Jake, the go-getter investor, diving into Dubai's real estate scene. He teams up with Mauro, the local real estate wizard, and the pair kick off a deal that's set to paint the city gold.

Contracts are signed at AED14.5m, cash talks have happened and Jake, the timing maestro, throws in a request for a 45-day contract extension—cue the suspense. Wait for it … a wildcard agent emerges, Moe, dangling a distressed deal at AED14m for a similar property that shakes Jake's commitment to Mauro. It's a plot twist that has Jake torn between loyalty and the allure of something new.

In a cinematic move, Jake approaches Mauro, suggesting a contract cancellation. However, the seller isn't letting go easily, brandishing the contract clauses like a shield: 8% of the selling price plus a 2% cut from Jake's deposit. Ouch.

Torn between loyalty and temptation, Jake makes the call. The original deal with Mauro moves forward, gears shifting toward the climax of ownership transfer. But hold onto your popcorn … In the distressed deal, a deceptive illusion unravels. The other owner was never actually selling, and the agent Moe was pulling strings in a distracting charade. There was no property for sale at 14m.

Dubai's skyline, the silent narrator of this real estate thriller, continues its ascent as Jake emerges, battle-tested, from the sands of property intrigue. The story unfolds in the city of dreams with ambition, tough choices and the relentless pursuit of the next big win.

Market Analysis

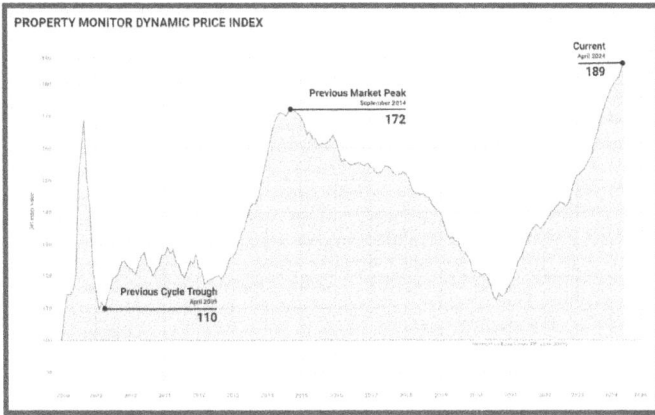

Figure 13. Property Monitor Dynamic Price Index
(Property Monitor, 2024)

Dubai's property market is on fire! The Property Monitor Dynamic Price Index reveals a current peak of 189 in April 2024, with an impressive year-over-year change of +20.07%. This surge reflects a robust market, driven by high demand and favourable conditions.

Now, let's see how Jake's story would have been different if he'd exercised due caution. He locked in a deal at AED14.5 million, but as the 45-day contract extension loomed, Moe, a wildcard agent, offered a distressed property (or rather, a mirage) at AED14 million. Torn, Jake finally committed to Mauro's original deal, sensing stability in a market showing consistent growth.

The data shows why Jake's decision was smart. Despite the temptation of a lower price, Dubai's market strength means secure investments often pay off. The index's rise from a previous cycle trough of 110 in 2009 to today's peak demonstrates resilience and growth.

With the property prices and transaction volumes on an upward trajectory, securing a deal now means locking in value before prices potentially soar even higher. Plus, dodging the hidden pitfalls of a too-good-to-be-true deal saves Jake from potential financial headaches and reinforces the value of trusted partnerships in real estate.

Conclusion

Dubai's skyline continues its majestic rise, much like Jake's investment portfolio. With the right moves, informed by the latest market data from Property Monitor, investors can navigate the thrilling twists of real estate and emerge victorious. So, gear up, stay informed, and let's make those smart, strategic moves in Dubai's dynamic real estate market!

PRO TIP !

In real estate, signing the contract demands certainty. Flashy distractions may sparkle, but they often mask unrealistic promises. When that ink dries, commitment is key. Stay focused, avoid the glitter and ensure your decisions are as solid as the foundations beneath those skyscrapers.

"The United Arab Emirates is not merely a financial or economic centre, nor is it only a tourist destination between East and West, but an important humanitarian centre on the international stage."*

—HIS HIGHNESS SHEIKH MOHAMMED BIN RASHID AL MAKTOUM

* https://sheikhmohammed.ae/en-us/quotes

CHAPTER 10

DUBAI OR NOT TO BUY:

Jaime's Ride Through Dubai
Real Estate

Jaime, a resident grappling with escalating post-COVID rent hikes, decided it was time to transition from being an annual renter to a property owner in Dubai. After securing pre-approval from a prominent bank, she and her husband delved into the real estate market, eventually settling on a family-friendly community and putting down a 10% security deposit for a property priced at AED2.8 million.

Anticipation hung in the air as they waited for the bank's final approval. However, when the valuation came through, reality hit hard: The property was appraised at AED2.6 million. A financial gap of AED200,000 loomed, sending Jaime into a state of agitation.

Seeking clarity, Jaime scrutinised the contract for possible exit strategies, but the MOU offered no solace. Frustration surfaced in a conversation with the agent as Jaime confronted the absence of crucial clauses that could have illuminated her options.

Caught in a dilemma, Jaime faced a tough decision: Cancelling the deal meant a 10% penalty, a substantial hit. On the other hand, proceeding with the purchase meant covering an additional amount that he hadn't anticipated.

In the harsh reality of Dubai's property market, Jaime found himself at a crossroads, grappling with financial implications and the potential derailment of his homeownership dreams. As the sands of uncertainty shifted beneath her, only time would reveal whether Jaime could navigate the intricacies of this unforeseen challenge.

Jaime somehow managed to borrow money from her family and decided to move ahead with the purchase. In spite of the hurdles, she is happy to live in a nice community in her own house.

Market Analysis

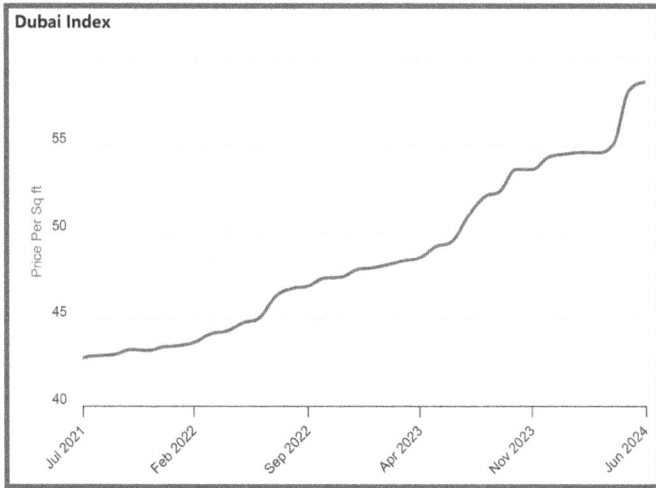

Figure 14 Rental Index July 2021-Jun 2024 *(Property Monitor, 2024)*

Dubai's rental market is sizzling, and the latest Rental Index graph says it all! Prices per square foot for both apartments and villas have been climbing steadily since July 2023. This surge reflects the vibrant demand and the city's unstoppable growth.

Now, let's dive into Jamie's journey. Jamie, fed up with sky-rocketing post-COVID rent hikes, decided to switch from renting to owning. She and her husband found their dream home in a family-friendly community, putting down a 10% deposit. But when the bank's valuation came in lower than expected, they faced a financial gap. Determined, Jamie borrowed money from family and sealed the deal.

The rising trend in the Rental Index highlights Jamie's savvy decision. As rental prices continue to soar, owning a property becomes an even smarter move. Jamie's quick action, despite the valuation hiccup, puts her in a prime position in a market where rents are only going up.

This data underscores the importance of making bold, informed decisions in a dynamic market. For Jamie and others eyeing homeownership, buying now not only offers stability but also shields against relentless rent increases. In Dubai's fast-paced real estate scene, being proactive and informed can turn obstacles into golden opportunities. So, gear up, make your move, and ride the wave of Dubai's booming market!

Conclusion

Families who have been renting houses in Dubai for five years or more are finally deciding to invest in property, inspired by the growing trend observed in Dubai's dynamic real estate landscape. Jaime's journey reflects this trend as he navigates the complexities of Dubai's property market. Despite facing challenges like appraisal discrepancies and contractual limitations, Jaime's determination to secure a property priced at AED2.8 million underscores the shifting dynamics of Dubai's real estate sector.

Jaime's story encapsulates the realities of Dubai's property market. As Jaime grapples with uncertainty, his journey underscores the importance of navigating the intricacies of real estate transactions in Dubai's evolving landscape. Against the backdrop of rising rental prices and increasing demand for homeownership, Jaime's experience serves as a microcosm of residents taking control of their housing destiny in the bustling city of Dubai. Dubai's rental market is buzzing with opportunity, offering investors a lucrative landscape to explore. It's time to seize the moment and ride the wave of Dubai's rental market growth!

PRO TIPS !

Clause Crusader: Agents are human (believe it or not), and details sometimes get overlooked. So, revisit that contract like a detective on a mission. Seek clarity and ask the tough questions.

Strategise, Don't Agonise: Yes, the 10% penalty sounds ominous, but don't let it paralyse you. It's a hurdle, not a roadblock. Crunch those numbers, explore creative financing options and strategise your way forward.

The Power of Persistence: Frustration is part of the game. Channel it into persistence. Keep pushing for answers, solutions and a pathway that aligns with your homeownership dreams.

Flexibility is Key: Real estate is a dynamic dance. Stay flexible and open-minded. If the script needs tweaking, be willing to adapt. It's your journey, after all. If you are not comfortable with paying additional 10% in the worst case scenario, make sure to inform your property advisor and add a suitable clause in the contract to avoid any penalties.

What lies in the heart of a buyer or seller is complicated. It could be the game of greed or the fear of missing out on a good deal. Whichever way you look at it, Dubai has seen its fair share of savvy investors lose their way.

PART III

INVESTORS

"All that glitters is not gold."

—WILLIAM SHAKESPEARE

CHAPTER 11

BAIT AND SWITCH IN THE CITY OF BLING:

Dubai's Real Estate Caper

In the glittering realm of Dubai's real estate market, Adam, drawn by the promise of a luxurious property, engaged with the ambitious owner, Lata, and the adept agent, Robert. The property, an extravagant villa valued at AED8.7 million, set the stage for a high-stakes transaction. After sealing the deal, they embarked on the bureaucratic journey to the developer for the NOC. Yet unbeknownst to Adam, lurking beneath the façade of opulence were overdue instalments and late fees totalling AED2.2 million.

When the developer unveiled the financial hurdles, Lata, seemingly unfazed, casually suggested that the burden should fall on Adam, the eager buyer. In the spirit of sealing the deal, Robert—hardly a master negotiator—convinced Adam to clear Lata's debts, ensuring the property remained under her name.

However, the glamour of Dubai real estate quickly tarnished. Lata, having secured her financial escape, abruptly reneged on the deal. With a casual promise of AED870,000, she vanished, leaving Adam and Robert stranded amid the gleaming skyscrapers. The ensuing legal battle was as tangled as Dubai's streets, with Robert and Adam persistently pursuing justice. A few months of courtroom dramas and several financial headaches later, victory was finally secured.

Amid the shadows of palm-fringed boulevards and architectural wonders, Adam's dreams were temporarily thwarted. The glittering city had, for a moment, concealed the complexities beneath its flawless surface.

Market Analysis

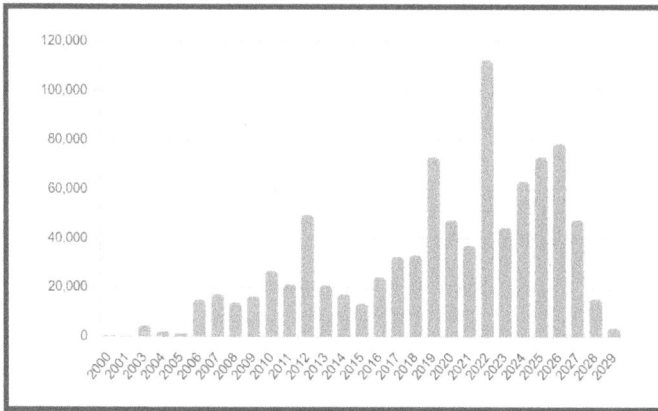

Figure 15. Total Units Completed by Year
(Graph created by using data from Property Monitor, 2024)

Dubai's property market is in overdrive! According to Property Monitor, the number of new units completed has soared, especially around 2020 and beyond. We're talking thousands of new homes hitting the market, signalling a bustling, competitive environment. But here's the kicker: Despite this boom in supply, it's still not enough to meet the surging demand from the influx of new residents and expats moving to Dubai.

The market data from Property Monitor paints a vivid picture: Even with the substantial completion of new units, the demand is outstripping supply. The influx of new residents and expats means properties are getting snapped up quickly, leaving room for potential financial oversights like the one Adam encountered.

In the high-stakes environment of Dubai real estate, due diligence is crucial. Adam's story highlights the need to dig deep into financial details, especially in a market where properties move fast and competition is fierce. With so many new units available, it's easy to assume the market is saturated, but the reality is quite the opposite.

Dubai's skyline is rising, and so are the opportunities.

Conclusion

In a bustling market, every second counts. It's tempting to leap at the chance for a steal-of-a-deal property, but in the frenzy, don't forget the golden rule: Haste makes waste. While speed is crucial, so is due diligence. Before you sign on the dotted line, ensure you have ticked all the boxes. As Adam's experience shows, navigating this market requires more than just ambition—it demands meticulous attention to detail and a strategic approach. So, gear up, stay vigilant, and make your mark in Dubai's ever-thriving real estate landscape!

PRO TIPS !

Know exactly what you should be looking for in your property dossier. Let's delve deeper:

1. **Oqood/Pre-title Deed/Title Deed**: These documents verify the ownership of the property and ensure that you are dealing with the rightful owner.
2. **ID of the Current Owner**: Confirming the identity of the current owner adds an extra layer of security to your transaction.
3. **Sale Purchase Agreement (SPA)**: Particularly important for off-plan properties in the resale market, the SPA ensures that what you are buying matches what is being presented by the agent or owner.
4. **Statement of Account**: If there's an ongoing payment plan with the developer, this document outlines the financial details, ensuring transparency and preventing any surprises down the line.

5. **Tenancy Contract**: For ready properties, reviewing the tenancy contract helps you understand any existing rental agreements in place.

6. **RERA Certificate of Your Agent**: Verifying RERA certification ensures that you are dealing with a licensed professional, offering you peace of mind throughout the transaction process.

Additionally, ensure that the current property owner has a UAE bank account, so you can prepare a manager's cheque for the final transfer in the trustee's office.

Remember, taking a meticulous approach now can save you from headaches and heartaches later. So, take your time, dot your i's, cross your t's … and happy house hunting!

If ever in doubt, you can reach out to me at jasmine@dubairealtycheck.com, so we can help you find solutions.

Picture this: Rohit's tale is a rollercoaster ride of twists and turns, waiting to grip you tighter than the city's sandstorms. But hold your breath, dear friend, for between these chapters lies a realm of secrets and surprises. What mysteries await in the shadows of Dubai's glittering skyline? Let's find out together!

"Trust, but verify."

—RONALD REAGAN

CHAPTER **12**

CRACKED DREAMS AND DELAYED SCHEMES:

Broken Promises in Dubai's
Property Market

A discerning businessman, Rohit found his attention captured by the myriad banners lining Sheikh Zayed Road, promising ambitious real estate ventures. Intrigued by the potential behind the advertisements, he wasted no time upon reaching his hotel, promptly calling the contact details provided. A meeting with the agent ensued, leading to a compelling pitch and a visit to the developer's sales centre, where Rohit was captivated by the allure of the show apartment. Convinced that he had stumbled upon a golden opportunity, he swiftly signed the contract and made the down payment.

Confident in the project's completion as construction began, Rohit's optimism dwindled over the years owing to persistent delays in the handover process. Days turned into weeks, months, and eventually years as the developer, like a master illusionist, continued pushing back deadlines. This prolonged delay planted seeds of distrust among Rohit and other buyers, casting doubts on the developer's ability to fulfil commitments.

When the much-anticipated day arrived for the property handover, it unfolded as a bittersweet moment. The formalities revealed a stark reality—damaged units, lacklustre furnishings and unsettling cracks on long-promised walls.

In the end, Rohit's journey, from the highs of anticipation to the lows of disappointment, mirrors the unpredictable dance of the Dubai property market. It's a narrative where dreams rest upon the shifting sands of time and trust, forcing investors to navigate the cracks in their once-rosy visions.

Analysis

Figure 16. Tilal Al Ghaf, by Majid Al Futtaim (2022)

If ever in doubt about where to invest, you can refer to this list of top developers shared below as these developers have proved their name in the Dubai real estate market.

List of top developers from Bayut (2003): https://www.bayut.com/mybayut/real-estate-developers-dubai/

- **EMAAR Properties**
- **Nakheel Properties**
- **Dubai Properties**
- **Meraas**

My personal favourite is Majid Al Futtaim, retail king of the UAE, who developed his first residential crystal lagoon community in the heart of Dubai, Tilal Al Ghaf. Guess what? They just launched another fabulous community called Ghaf Woods in Dubai! While Tilal Al Ghaf is their first foray into residential living in Dubai, they've already made waves with other incredible communities in Sharjah, Muscat, Oman, and Beirut. It's like they're taking over the whole region, one stunning development at a time!

Conclusion

Rohit's journey serves as a vivid snapshot of Dubai's unpredictable property market, underscoring the need for meticulous due diligence in the realm of real estate investments. Remember, it's not just about the deal; it's also about mastering the nuances and thriving in the face of unexpected challenges.

PRO TIPS !

When venturing into real estate, especially in a dynamic market like Dubai, blending enthusiasm with a healthy dose of caution is crucial. Here are some key pieces of advice inspired by Rohit's story:

1. **Research, Research, Research:** Thoroughly research the developer before signing contracts or making down payments. Investigate their track record, their reviews from previous buyers and their history of completing projects on time.
2. **Visit the Site:** Don't rely solely on glossy brochures and show apartments. Take the time to visit the construction site, inspect the progress and get a realistic view of what you are investing in.
3. **Stay Sceptical:** While optimism is great, it is essential to maintain a healthy dose of scepticism. If a deal seems too good to be true, it might be worth a second, more critical look.

4. **Network and Seek Advice:** Connect with other investors, especially those with experience in the local market. Their insights and experiences can provide valuable guidance and help you make more informed decisions.

5. **Patience Pays Off:** Real estate investments often require a long-term perspective. Be patient and understand that delays and challenges are part of the process. Rushed decisions can lead to disappointment.

Remember, while the potential for profit in real estate is significant, it is essential to approach each investment with a combination of optimism and pragmatism to ensure a more rewarding and less turbulent journey.

Checklist–Preparing for Property Handover

☐ Schedule a final inspection of the property.
☐ Ensure all agreed-upon repairs are completed.*
☐ Verify that all utilities (water, electricity, gas) are connected.
☐ Check that all fixtures and fittings are in place.
☐ Obtain the property handover documents.
☐ Make the final payment and settle any outstanding dues.
☐ Collect all keys, access cards, and manuals.
☐ Update your address with relevant authorities.
☐ Plan the move and arrange for movers if necessary.
☐ Celebrate your new property and settle in!
☐ Hire a snagging company. (Email us for suggestions.)

**Scan to View
Complete Checklist**

"The truth is rarely pure and never simple."

—OSCAR WILDE

CHAPTER 13

THE SNEAKY SEVEN:

Where Apartments Multiply,
but Agents Disappear

In the intriguing narrative of Mr Ahmed's Dubai real estate journey, he found himself fielding a daily deluge of calls from various agents, each vying for his attention with different property pitches. Amid this whirlwind, he navigated the suggestions put forth by the experienced Stella and the dynamic Rachel.

Initially captivated by the allure of Al Jadaf and its promising returns, the plot thickened when Rachel, the risk-taker, presented the alternative allure of Arjan, backed by a tempting discount from a new developer. After a methodical month of weighing his options, Mr Ahmed opted for diversification, committing to seven apartments based on Rachel's promise of a 3% discount post her 4% commission.

Wise to the ways of the real estate world, Mr Ahmed demanded written confirmation for added assurance, and Rachel swiftly delivered through an email from her private domain. However, the climax took an unexpected twist as Rachel seemingly vanished into the Dubai skyline after Mr Ahmed parted ways with 24% of his investment.

Market Analysis

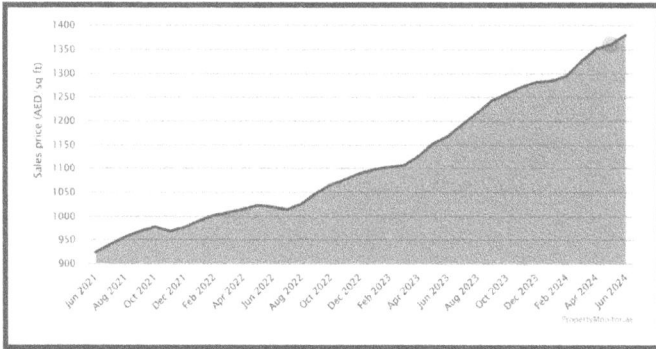

Figure 17. Dubai City Index Scale 2021–2024
(Property Monitor, 2024)

Based on Property Monitor's data, the real estate market has experienced a notable surge in transactions, reflecting heightened investor confidence. This positive trend can be attributed to the Dubai Government's consistent endeavours to improve regulatory frameworks and investment environments. In particular, the off-plan market has played a crucial role in propelling real estate growth in both Abu Dhabi and Dubai, with expectations of sustained increases in sales transactions and overall value in the foreseeable future. Buying off-plan properties in Dubai is a very smooth process, especially preferred by international buyers since they don't need to be physically present.

Conclusion

Thus concludes the dramatic chapter in Mr Ahmed's real estate venture, painted with the brush strokes of viewings, incessant calls, strategic decisions and the pursuit of a golden opportunity in the thriving Dubai market. What you can take from this experience is a better understanding of how miscommunications can lead to costly situations.

PRO TIP !

This tale serves as a canvas for a pearl of wisdom: In real estate, communication is the cornerstone. Always put everything in writing to ensure clarity and avoid surprises. While diversification can be a smart move, never lose sight of the fundamental importance of trust and commitment in every deal. In the City of Gold, every opportunity deserves a strategic approach.

"Lost time is never found again."

—BENJAMIN FRANKLIN

CHAPTER 14

DIRHAMS IN DISTRESS:

Mark's Million-Dollar Misadventure

In the dazzling realm of Dubai's real estate, Mark, a global buyer hungry for a piece of the city's luxurious skyline, set his sights on a property worth a cool AED15.2 million. Eager to make this dream a reality, he inked the deal with a 10% deposit, the promise of opulent living shimmering in the desert sun.

But here's where the script takes an unexpected twist. The international dance of funds transfer, a complex ballet governed by financial regulations, tripped Mark into a bureaucratic tango. The one-month validity on the contract quickly turned into a ticking time bomb.

As Mark grappled with the intricacies of moving money across borders, the sands of Dubai's timepiece slipped away mercilessly. Weeks melted like an ice-cream cone in the desert heat, with the contract's expiration date becoming a looming spectre in Mark's real estate saga.

In a frenzied finale, Mark managed to hit 'Send' on the funds transfer, but the damage was done. The contract, now a relic of the past, invoked a clause that allowed the seller to pocket 10% of the property's value—a staggering AED1,520,000—as compensation for the dance that never reached the final chord.

Dubai's skyline, once tantalisingly close, now seemed like a mirage in the rearview mirror. Mark's journey, painted with the strokes of delay, became a cautionary tale. In the swagger-filled corridors of international real estate, it served as a reminder that, in the pursuit of dreams, mastering the choreography of cross-border transactions is as crucial as the keys to the property itself.

As Mark counted the cost, his story echoed through the skyscrapers and bustling streets of Dubai, a symphony of caution narrated in the inimitable style of real estate tales, where the currency of time can be as valuable as the dirhams exchanged in pursuit of the city's coveted addresses.

Market Analysis

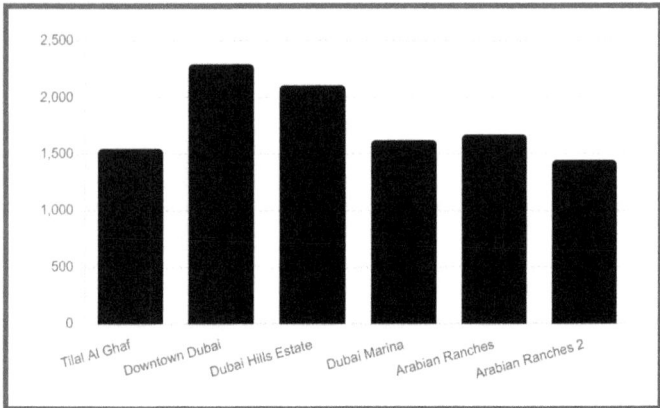

Figure 18. Median Price/sft – June 2024
(Property Monitor, 2024)

Dubai's real estate market is hotter than ever! Property Monitor's latest data shows soaring median prices per square foot in top areas like Tilal Al Ghaf, Downtown Dubai, Dubai Hills, Dubai Marina, Arabian Ranches, and Arabian Ranches 2. These prime locations are the epicentre of luxury living, reflecting the intense demand and vibrant market dynamics.

For investors like Mark, who set his sights on a luxurious AED15.2 million property, this market is a goldmine. But it's not just about picking the right property—it's about mastering the timing. With median prices climbing, the competition is fierce. Mark's journey through the complex dance of international fund transfers serves as a cautionary tale. The ticking time bomb of a one-month contract validity emphasizes the importance of swift, strategic moves.

In a market where prime areas are seeing such significant price growth, delays can be costly. Mark's experience underscores the critical need to navigate financial transactions with precision. The stakes are high, but so are the rewards. In Dubai's fast-paced real estate scene, being prepared and acting quickly can make all the difference between securing a dream property and facing costly setbacks.

Conclusion

Understandably, you are excited to jump into a Dubai real estate market that's full of profits, but timing is key! As you aim to seize the right opportunity and enjoy the returns, don't forget about aligning your timeline with the contracts. After all, a well-timed investment is a smart investment.

PRO TIPS !

Let's talk contracts!

Contracts: When securing a home in the secondary market, you will encounter three separate contracts:

1. Contract A between the agency and seller
2. Contract B between the buyer and agency
3. Contract F, also known as the MOU.

Here's the scoop: All these contracts are generated online on the DLD website. The buyer/seller receives an email as well as an SMS to review and accept/decline the contract. After signing Contract A and B, both contracts are merged into Contract F by the agency on the Dubai Land Department website.

While signing Contract F/MOU, a deposit cheque is collected from the buyer. This MOU sets the stage with a 10% deposit cheque to the agency (not the seller, mind you). But don't worry, it's not cashed—it's returned on the final transfer date unless something goes wrong, like the buyer backing out from the deal. Typically, you'll agree on a timeline, say 30 days for cash deals or 60 days for mortgages. And hey, delays happen (such as third-party delays caused by banks or developers issuing NOCs), so watch out for those contract extensions—usually 7–15 days if you've got the right clauses in place.

Always consider your contract timeline and ensure the clauses align with your goals and feasibility. It's the fine print that makes all the difference!

And now let's look at the other side of the coin (unspaced em dash) the seller's perspective.

Checklist–Investing in Dubai Real Estate

- ☐ Set clear investment goals.
- ☐ Research high-growth areas in Dubai.
- ☐ Analyse market trends and data.
- ☐ Calculate the potential return on investment (ROI).
- ☐ Understand the risks involved.
- ☐ Diversify your real estate portfolio.
- ☐ Choose properties with high rental yield.
- ☐ Consider the long-term appreciation potential.
- ☐ Work with a knowledgeable real estate advisor.
- ☐ Review and update your investment strategy regularly.

**Scan to View
Complete Checklist**

Ladies and gentlemen, gather 'round! Are you ready to uncover the thrilling secrets lurking within the dazzling realm of Dubai's real estate market? Picture this: A world where million-dirham deals hinge on the flip of a coin, where every handshake hides a web of intrigue and where fortunes are made and lost in the blink of an eye. But beware, my dear friend, not everything is as it seems. Are you brave enough to venture forth and unlock the mysteries that lie ahead?

PART IV

SELLERS

"One day, in retrospect, the years of struggle will strike you as the most beautiful."

—SIGMUND FREUD

CHAPTER 15

LIES, LISTINGS, AND LAUGHTER:

Rebecca's Dubai Debacle

In the glittering heart of Dubai, where skyscrapers touched the clouds and dreams were sold with every sunrise, Rebecca found herself at the mercy of the city's pulse. The lush greenery in the middle of the dessert framed her luxury villa, a haven she believed to be her sanctuary, until Daniel, a smooth-talking real estate agent, stepped into her life with whispers of a secret.

With the urgency of a ticking clock, Daniel painted a vivid tale of an impending market bubble, a clandestine narrative only he claimed to know. Fear gripped Rebecca's heart as he warned her of looming financial disaster, advising her to offload her property before the bubble burst. In the dimly lit corner of a posh cafe, with hushed tones and a gaze that hinted at classified information, Daniel convinced Rebecca to part with her haven.

The deal was struck at AED2.5 million in Tilal Al Ghaf, a price that seemed like a lifeline in the face of a supposed market collapse. Yet unbeknownst to Rebecca, this was the beginning of her descent into a labyrinth of deception.

Figure 19. Crystal lagoon in Tilal Al Ghaf, 2024

Weeks later, Dubai's real estate market laughed in the face of Daniel's prophecies. Properties in Rebecca's coveted neighbourhood skyrocketed, but her former townhouse was lost in the shadows of regret, sold for a sum far beneath its true value.

As the city sparkled with the prosperity Rebecca missed out on, regret gnawed at her soul. But she didn't give up: after two years, she bought a bigger villa in the same community.

Daniel faced the consequences of his cunning narrative. Yet, the tale didn't end there. Rebecca became a symbol of resilience, her story a beacon of caution for those enticed by the lustrous promises of Dubai's real estate dreams.

Amid the gleaming towers and bustling streets, Rebecca's narrative echoed through the city, urging others to navigate the glittering real estate landscape with vigilance, scepticism and an unwavering resolve to unveil the truth.

Market Analysis

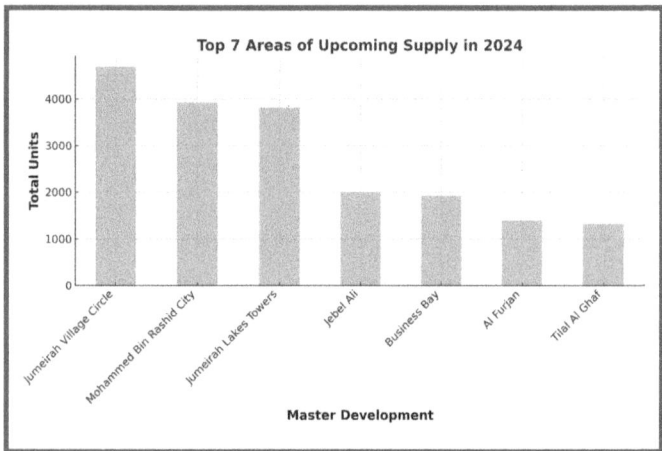

Top 7 Areas of Upcoming Supply in 2024

Figure 20. Top 7 Areas with Upcoming Supply in Dubai
(Based on the data from Property Monitor, 2024)

The Dubai real estate market is sizzling, and if you're not already in the game, it's time to get moving. According to the *Khaleej Times*, property prices and rentals are set to rise until 2025, driven by a population boom that's outpacing new property supply by 300%! Can you believe that?

Now, let's dive into the details and see why this market is so hot right now:

1. **Units Launched vs. Handed Over:** In 2023, Dubai saw a whopping 100,000 units launched, but only 40,000 are expected to be handed over in 2024. That means the demand for ready homes is skyrocketing! Developers are working around the clock to meet this demand, but the market is moving faster than they can keep up.

2. **Impact of FATF Grey List Removal:** Here's a game-changer. In February 2024, the UAE was removed from the Financial Action Task Force's (FATF) Grey List. This boosted investor confidence big time, making Dubai a hot spot for foreign investments. Investors are flocking to the market, driving demand through the roof.

3. **Luxury Segment Resilience:** Despite initial predictions of a market slowdown, the luxury segment is thriving. High net worth individuals from the US, Canada, and other markets are snapping up properties, keeping prices and rentals on an upward trajectory. The high-end market is stronger than ever!

4. **Supply Challenges and Future Projections:** New projects are being launched at a breakneck pace—one every 18 hours! Yet, the supply of ready homes still lags behind. Over the next five years, we expect the supply to catch up, but until then, prices are likely to remain high due to the limited supply.

5. **Transaction Trends:** The first quarter of 2024 shattered records with 34,000 transactions—a 20% increase from the previous year. Off-plan properties dominated, making up 58% of all transactions. End-users and investors alike see off-plan as the best bet right now.

6. **Price Trends:** Demand for properties priced between AED3–5 million surged by 2.6% in March. Villa prices in key communities jumped by 11% to 38%, and apartment prices rose by 7% to 29%. The market is on fire!

As per the above graph from Property Monitor, you can study the Top Locations with Upcoming Supply. These areas are primed for significant development, offering fantastic opportunities for buyers and investors.

Rebecca sold her villa in Tilal Al Ghaf for AED2.5 million, fearing a market downturn that never came. Fast forward, and the market exploded! Prices in her neighbourhood soared, reflecting the current trend. Rebecca's tale is a powerful reminder of the importance of understanding market dynamics and seizing the right opportunities.

Just like Rebecca learned, you need to stay ahead of the curve. The market is dynamic, and the right moves can lead to incredible gains. So, whether you're buying, selling, or investing, now is the time to act. The Dubai real estate market is booming, and the opportunities are endless!

Conclusion

In the whirlwind of Dubai's real estate scene, Rebecca's tale of deception and redemption is a gripping reminder to investors and dreamers alike. As skyscrapers touch the clouds and dreams are sold with every sunrise, it's easy to get swept away by the allure of the city's promises. But behind every glittering façade lies a cautionary tale, urging us to tread carefully and seek truth amid the glamour.

PRO TIP !

Remember to keep your wits about you when navigating Dubai's real estate rollercoaster. Don't let the shiny promises blindside you. Conduct thorough research, ask the tough questions and *always* trust your instincts. In a city where dreams are sold like hotcakes, it pays to be savvy, sceptical and always ready to separate fact from fiction. After all, in the land of skyscrapers and sand, the only certainty is the unpredictability of the market.

"Opportunity does not knock; it presents itself when you beat down the door."

—KYLE CHANDLER

CHAPTER 16

DUBAI LISTINGS AND A REGRETTABLE MISSING QUEST FOR THE PERFECT DEAL

In the bustling streets of Dubai, Mr Ibrahim found himself caught in the symphony of the city's real estate market. His phone buzzed incessantly, besieged by tenacious agents vying for the chance to list his property. An ocean of promises flooded his ears, each agent claiming to fetch a higher price than the last.

Amid the cacophony, one agent stood out: a seasoned professional named Rachel. Her knowledge about the market was like a breath of fresh air, cutting through the noise with facts and figures. Intrigued, Mr Ibrahim allowed himself to entertain the idea of selling his property.

As he contemplated the decision, Rachel worked tirelessly to provide him with a comprehensive understanding of the market. Armed with a detailed report from Property Monitor, she demonstrated recent transactions and market trends, anchoring Mr Ibrahim's expectations in reality.

Driven by a pressing need to fund his daughter's university education, Mr Ibrahim reluctantly decided to sell. With unwavering dedication, Rachel managed to secure a reasonable offer of AED4.2 million, aligning closely with recent transactions in the area. She emphasised the importance of acting swiftly in the dynamic market.

However, Mr Ibrahim hesitated. Fuelled by higher-priced promises, other agents had convinced him to hold out for a better deal. As he explored these tempting alternatives, precious time slipped through his fingers.

A week later, when Mr Ibrahim finally acknowledged the reality of market prices, he discovered the buyer Rachel had diligently secured had moved on. The opportunity to sell at a reasonable AED4.2 million was lost.

Regret washed over him as the urgency to secure funds intensified. Mr Ibrahim, recognising the gravity of his mistake, had to eventually sell his property at a much lower price—a piffling AED4 million—that was less than the market value Rachel had initially secured.

The echoes of missed opportunities lingered as Mr Ibrahim grappled with the consequences of indecision. The tale of his journey through Dubai's real estate market became cautionary, teaching others that sometimes the highest offer isn't the best offer and time lost in hesitation can have a steep price tag.

Market Analysis

Hey there, savvy investors! Let's talk about the hottest apps in town for keeping your finger on the pulse of Dubai's real estate market:

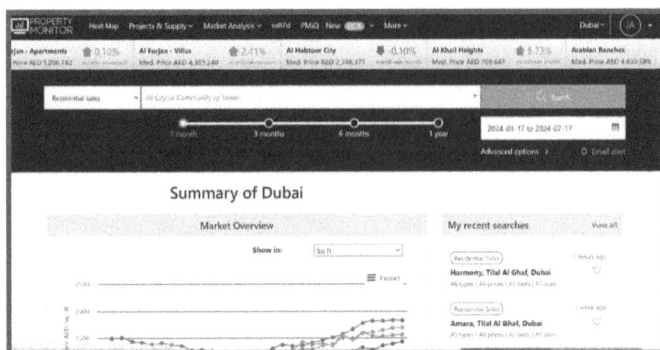

1. **Dubai Rest:** Imagine having all your property needs in one handy app. From browsing listings to checking out neighbourhoods, Dubai Rest has got it covered. Plus, it throws in nifty tools like mortgage calculators to sweeten the deal.

2. **Property Monitor:** Looking for the inside scoop on property trends? Look no further than Property Monitor. Dive deep into market data, spot trends before they hit the headlines and make smart investment moves like a pro.

3. **2GIS:** While you're out and about, why not let 2GIS guide you? It's a mapping app, but it's also your secret weapon for scoping out property locations, nearby amenities and all the hotspots in town.

4. **Property Finder:** Hunting for your next big investment? Property Finder is your go-to guru. With a treasure trove of listings, detailed property descriptions and even virtual tours, finding your dream property is a breeze.

5. **Bayut**: Last but not least, Bayut is your trusty side-kick in the real estate game. It's packed with listings, handy valuation and mortgage comparison tools and insider tips to help you stay ahead of the curve.

So, there you have it, folks! With these indispensable apps in your arsenal, you'll be ruling the real estate scene in Dubai in no time. Happy investing!

Conclusion

In the vibrant mosaic of Dubai's real estate hustle, Mr Ibrahim's rollercoaster journey reads like a gripping tale from a suspense novel. Amid the cacophony of agents' promises and the siren song of higher offers, he found himself caught in a whirlwind of uncertainty. But fear not, dear friend, for in every twist and turn lies a nugget of wisdom and perhaps a chuckle or two.

Who could forget Rachel, the beacon of sanity in Mr Ibrahim's stormy sea of choices? With her trusty side-kick, Property Monitor, she wielded market insights like a wizard with a wand, grounding our protagonist in the cold, hard reality of Dubai's real estate scene. But alas, even her sage advice couldn't shield Mr Ibrahim from the temptations of greener pastures.

And oh! The allure of those elusive perfect deals! Like a mirage in the desert, they shimmered tantalisingly on the horizon, promising riches beyond imagination. But as Mr Ibrahim soon discovered, chasing shadows only leads to a sunburned nose and an empty wallet.

In the end, our hero learned a valuable lesson: Sometimes, the grass isn't greener on the other side—it's just painted that way. So, dear reader, heed his tale and ask yourself: Is it worth risking a bird in the hand for two in the bush? Or should we embrace the imperfect beauty of the here and now?

PRO TIPS !

1. **Ride the Tech Wave:** Dive into the world of real estate apps like a pro surfer catching the perfect wave. Dubai Rest, DXB Interact/Property Monitor, 2GIS, Property Finder and Bayut are your trusty surfboards, guiding you through the ebbs and flows of the market. Hang ten on the crest of data-driven insights and ride the tide of success straight to the shore of your dreams.

2. **Trust, but Verify:** Like a wise old owl, listen to Rachel's advice ... but don't forget to do your own homework. Dive deep into the murky waters of market trends and recent transactions. Who knows what hidden treasures you might uncover?

3. **Time is Money, Honey:** In the fast-paced world of real estate, hesitation is the enemy. Like a ninja with a stopwatch, act swiftly and decisively. The early bird gets the worm, or in Mr Ibrahim's case, the AED4.2 million offer.

4. **Laugh in the Face of Regret:** When life hands you lemons, make lemonade, add a splash of humour and raise a toast to the absurdity of it all. After all, what's a little regret between friends?

"A successful man is one who can lay a firm foundation with the bricks others have thrown at him."

—DAVID BRINKLEY

CHAPTER 17

VILLA VANISHES:

The 59-day Drama in Dubai's
Property Playground

In the hustle of Dubai's property game, Mr Mohamed faced a cash crunch, prompting a bold move. His prized villa (under construction), a hot commodity in a golf club community, hit the market at a jaw-dropping AED7.25 million, a deal sweet enough to attract the savvy eye of overseas buyer Mr Ramesh.

As the paperwork dance unfolded, a 60-day contract (MOU or Contract F) was drafted, setting the stage for a high-stakes negotiation. Feeling the pressure of a ticking clock, Mohamed pressed Ramesh to fast-track the cash transfer, but the buyer seemed to be on a different timeline.

The climax hit on the 59th day when Ramesh finally rolled in for the cash transfer. Little did he know, Mohamed had already pulled a real estate Houdini, securing funds elsewhere. Unfortunately, Mr Mohamed was allegedly sick and hospitalised—and Mohamed vanished from the deal.

Ramesh, perhaps sensing the consequences of his own delays, opted not to unleash the legal hounds. Meanwhile, Mohamed, seizing the opportunity, flipped the villa the very next day for the staggering amount of AED7.6 million.

Market Analysis

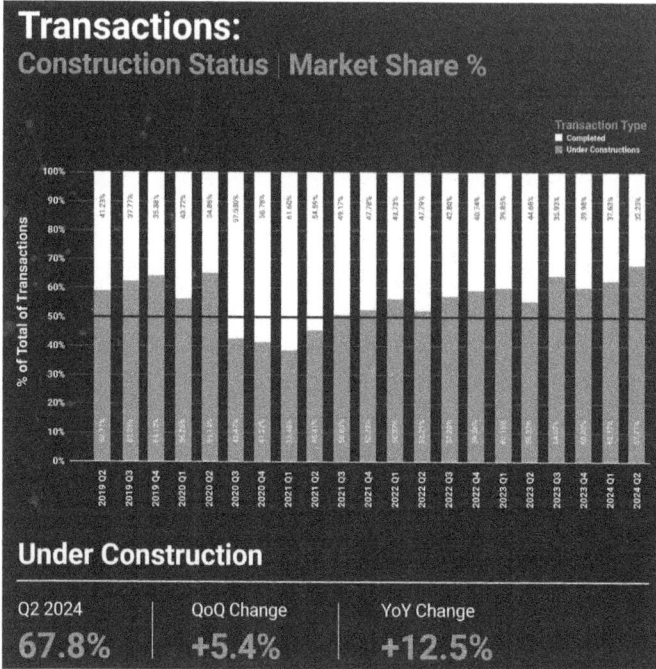

Figure 21. Construction Status | Market Share
(Property Monitor, 2024)

Dubai's real estate market is on fire, and the latest graph from Property Monitor tells it all! From Q2 2019 to Q2 2024, the percentage of under-construction property transactions has skyrocketed, hitting a whopping 67.8%! That's right, folks—developers are racing against time, and investors are diving into these projects with a

+12.5% year-on-year increase. Why? Because they know the future value is just too good to pass up!

This surge in under-construction transactions highlights a significant shift in market dynamics, reflecting growing investor confidence and the anticipation of future price appreciation. Importantly, these transactions are not only direct purchases from developers but also include the resale of off-plan properties. Investors are capitalizing on the market's momentum, flipping their off-plan investments for substantial gains even before the projects are completed.

As the demand for off-plan properties continues to rise, the limited supply of new homes only adds fuel to the fire. This trend underscores the fast-paced, high-stakes nature of Dubai's property market, where strategic timing and savvy investments can lead to significant rewards.

In the context of such a vibrant market, the story of Mr. Mohamed and Mr. Ramesh becomes even more compelling. Their high-stakes deal, filled with delays and last-minute manoeuvres, exemplifies the kind of rapid decision-making and strategic moves that define Dubai's real estate landscape.

Conclusion

Contracts should match the urgency of the situation, not some standard 60-day template. In a fast-paced market, keep cash-to-cash deals to 30 days and be clear about payment details. Also, cover bases for potential delays, such as banks or NOC transfers, in additional clauses. In this real estate drama, it's less about promises and more about pacts.

> **PRO TIPS !**
>
> In a world of high-stakes real estate, while the market is moving so fast in Dubai, this is a reminder that success isn't just about square footage and views; it's also about mastering the art of timing and negotiation. Now, go out there and make your real estate moves count.

In the intricate tapestry of real estate, the devil truly lies in the details. Yet, amidst the chaos, transparency prevails as the guiding light, illuminating the path to wisdom and ensuring that every setback becomes a stepping stone to a brighter future.

CHAPTER 18

MUTUAL RESET:

Ankita Scrapped the
AED7.9 Million Deal

In the colourful tapestry of real estate, Ankita crossed paths with a new agent, Jennifer, whose helpful and remarkably transparent reputation preceded her. As the duo embarked on a quest for the perfect property, Jennifer swiftly lived up to her stellar reputation.

She unveiled a gem: A property in Tilal Al Ghaf exclusively listed at AED7.9 million with an agent in her company, a rare find in a market where comparable homes were commanding prices of AED8.1 million and beyond. The deal seemed like a golden ticket, and Ankita and her family eagerly embraced the opportunity.

Figure 22. Amenities in Elan, Tilal Al Ghaf

The initial stages were smooth sailing—an enticing offer, an MOU signed and promises of a layout that mirrored Ankita's vision. However, when the time came to apply for the NOC (No Objection Certificate) and finalise the SPA(Sale Purchase Agreement), a chink in the armour revealed itself. The layout outlined in the original booking agreement with the developer, showcasing a bedroom downstairs as Ankita desired, diverged from the blueprint presented during the subsequent paperwork shuffle.

Ankita directed her fury at Jennifer, the agent who had initially seemed like a beacon of reliability. Amid the chaos, Jennifer sought counsel from Hamad, a seasoned agent on the seller's side with a decade of experience. Together, they unravelled the mystery: A simple administrative mistake had created this discrepancy.

Realising the gravity of the situation and fuelled by a commitment to transparency, both Jennifer and Hamad approached Ankita with the unfortunate truth. Acknowledging the honest error, they collectively decided to call off the deal with the seller's agreement.

As the dust settled, lessons emerged. The property game, intricate and unforgiving, taught Jennifer a valuable truth: The devil is in the details. With a wiser perspective, Ankita, Jennifer and Hamad parted ways amicably with the deal cancelled, but bridges unburned.

In the aftermath, the property found a new suitor, and with the increasing demand for the Tilal Al Ghaf community, the seller fetched an even higher price of AED8.3 million a month later. The narrative etched a lesson into Jennifer's real estate journey: Meticulous scrutiny of documents and exhaustive detailing in contracts could be the fine line between a dream deal and a bitter disappointment. A chapter closed, but wisdom gained for those navigating the ever-evolving landscape of real estate.

Market Analysis

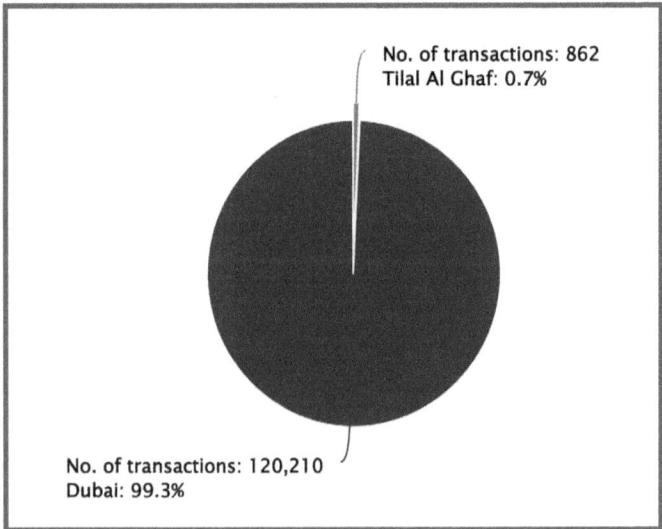

No. of transactions: 862
Tilal Al Ghaf: 0.7%

No. of transactions: 120,210
Dubai: 99.3%

Figure 23. Sales Volume, Tilal Al Ghaf vs Dubai in 2023
(Property Monitor, 2023)

According to data from Property Monitor, the Tilal Al Ghaf community in Dubai remains competitively priced compared with many other communities in the area. In 2023, Tilal Al Ghaf secured a 0.7% market share of overall Dubai, which is amongst the UAE's top 11 communities, indicating its growing popularity and demand among investors and homebuyers alike. Renowned for its crystal lagoon and high demand, Tilal Al Ghaf has proven to be a lucrative investment opportunity for many, yielding substantial profits for investors while ensuring satisfaction for residents.

During floods in Dubai, Tilal Al Ghaf demonstrated resilience and superior construction quality compared with other communities, reaffirming the decent build quality maintained by Majid Al Futtaim, the developer behind the project. Leveraging its reputation as the retail leader in the UAE, Majid Al Futtaim utilises top-notch materials and engages renowned architects and interior designers such as SOATA and Kelly Hoppens. This commitment to excellence enables Majid Al Futtaim to deliver unparalleled design and create thriving communities like Tilal Al Ghaf.

Conclusion

Navigating real estate demands more than just numbers and signatures; it also requires a keen eye for detail and a readiness to pivot when unexpected obstacles arise. For Jennifer, Ankita and all those entwined in this narrative, the takeaway is clear: Transparency, communication and a proactive approach to ironing out potential discrepancies are paramount. In a field where every detail matters, ensuring that contracts reflect the true essence of a deal can be the difference between a dream realised and a deal derailed.

As the story closes, it leaves behind not just a cancelled deal but a legacy of insight and wisdom. It serves as a reminder that in the ever-shifting landscape of real estate, those who emerge with lessons learned and resilience intact are well-equipped for the next chapter in this thrilling, unpredictable journey.

PRO TIPS !

Embarking on a real estate journey is akin to navigating uncharted waters. To thrive in this dynamic realm, consider the following advice:

1. **Detail is Key:** Scrutinise every document with meticulous attention. From initial agreements to official paperwork, ensure that every detail aligns with your vision.

2. **Transparent Communication:** Foster open and honest communication with your real estate agent. Discuss your expectations, preferences and any concerns upfront to avoid surprises down the line.

3. **Lesson from Ankita and Jennifer:** Ankita and Jennifer's story teaches us that even with the best intentions, discrepancies can arise. Be adaptable, responsive and ready to reassess if unexpected challenges emerge.

4. **Craft Clear Contracts:** Work with your agent to create contracts that are not only legally sound but also comprehensively reflect the terms of your agreement. Be explicit about layouts, timelines and any crucial details.

5. **Educate Yourself**: Stay informed about the local real estate market. Understanding current trends, pricing dynamics and potential pitfalls empowers you to make well-informed decisions.

6. **Build a Supportive Team**: Surround yourself with a reliable team, including a knowledgeable agent, legal counsel and financial advisors. Their expertise can be invaluable in navigating the complexities of real estate.

7. **Patience and Persistence**: Real estate transactions often involve twists and turns. Patience and persistence are virtues that can help you weather the storms and capitalise on unexpected opportunities.

Remember, the real estate journey is not just about securing a property; it's about creating a home and an investment for your future. Approach it with a strategic mindset, a keen eye for detail and an openness to adapt when needed. Your dream property may be just around the corner, waiting for you to navigate the path wisely.

Checklist–Steps to Selling Your Property

- ☐ Determine the market value of your property.
- ☐ Choose a reputable real estate agent.
- ☐ Prepare your property for viewing (cleaning, repairs, staging).
- ☐ Gather all necessary documents (title deed, NOC from developer).
- ☐ List your property on multiple platforms for maximum exposure.
- ☐ Screen potential buyers for serious interest.
- ☐ Negotiate offers and terms of sale.
- ☐ Draft and review the sales agreement.
- ☐ Complete the necessary legal formalities.
- ☐ Ensure a smooth handover of the property to the buyer.

**Scan to View
Complete Checklist**

Checklist–Avoiding Common Pitfalls

- ☐ Always conduct a property inspection before purchasing.
- ☐ Verify the authenticity of property documents.
- ☐ Be aware of hidden costs (maintenance fees, service charges).
- ☐ Understand the terms of your mortgage.
- ☐ Ensure there are no outstanding dues on the property.
- ☐ Check for any legal disputes involving the property.
- ☐ Avoid properties with unclear or disputed titles.
- ☐ Make sure the property complies with local regulations.
- ☐ Seek advice from legal and real estate professionals.
- ☐ Have a contingency plan in case of unforeseen issues.

**Scan to View
Complete Checklist**

IN THE END, IS THIS ALL WORTH IT?

Alright, listen up because this is the wild rollercoaster ride through Dubai's real estate that will make your head spin and your heart race. Against all odds, these gutsy folks decided to flip the script on the nightmare scenario and turn it into a blockbuster success story. I'm talking about owning a piece of Dubai, folks!

Picture this: Deceptive listings, unexpected hurdles and more twists than a Hollywood plot. These warriors did not back down; they faced those challenges like superheroes in a comic book. And guess what? They're not just homeowners now—they are the kings and queens of their own Dubai castles.

Ask them if it was worth it, and you'll get a resounding 'Hell yeah!' The battles, the drama and the moments that had them on the edge—it's all part of the epic journey that led them to seize the keys of their dream homes.

So, if you're on the brink of diving into the real estate madness, let these rockstars be your inspiration. Don't let the nightmares scare you off; instead, let them fuel your fire. Because, my friends, pursuing your dream home is a blockbuster adventure waiting to happen.

And in the immortal words of real estate guru Andrew Carnegie, 'Ninety percent of all millionaires become so through owning real estate' (Investing.com, 2022). These folks, now living the dream, are living proof that real estate can be your ticket to the millionaire's club amid the chaos.

So, grab your popcorn, buckle up and get ready for the quirkiest, most thrilling ride of your life. Here's to the bold ones who turned their real estate nightmares into a chart-topping blockbuster! Cheers to the dreamers and the dealmakers!

Congratulations on reaching the end of this wild ride through the Dubai real estate jungle! You are now armed with the knowledge and savvy judgement to navigate this dynamic landscape like a pro.

But wait, there's more!

As a special token of appreciation for our intrepid readers, we are offering free consultations, free home valuation and a whopping 11% discount on agency fees for the first 111 lucky ones who seize this opportunity.

So don't hesitate—Send an email to jasmine@dubai realtycheck.com, and let's kickstart your real estate adventure together!

https://www.dubairealtycheck.com/

REFERENCES

20 Famous Real Estate Investing Quotes. (n.d.). *Realty Mogul.* https://www.realtymogul.com/knowledge-center/article/20-famous-real-estate-investing-quotes

'90% of all millionaires become so through owning real-estate'. (2022, March 17). *Investing.com.* https://in.investing.com/news/90-of-all-millionaires-become-so-through-owning-realestate-3125374

Abbas, W. (2024, April 28). Dubai: Why property prices, rentals will continue to rise next year also. *Khaleej Times.* https://www.khaleejtimes.com/uae/dubai-why-property-prices-rentals-will-continue-to-rise-next-year-also

Al Maktoum, M. B. R. (2013). *Flashes of Thought.* Dubai: Motivate Publishing.

Dubai Real Estate Market Statistics. (2024). *Property Monitor.* https://propertymonitor.ae/v2/dubai-real-estate-market-statistics.php

'Experience of working with real estate agents in Dubai – Survey results'. (2024, March). *My Bayut.*

https://www.bayut.com/mybayut/survey-result-sexperience-real-estate-agents-dubai/

Halligan, N. (2024, February 16). Have Dubai property prices reached their peak? *The National News: Business.* https://www.thenationalnews.com/business/property/2024/02/16/dubai-property-prices-not-close-to-peak-yet-although-growth-slowing/

Quotes by His Highness Sheikh Mohammed Bin Rashid Al Maktoum. (n.d.). *Website of His Highness Sheikh Mohammed Bin Rashid Al Maktoum.* https://sheikhmohammed.ae/en-us/quotes

Quotes by Mohammed bin Rashid Al Maktoum. (n.d.). *Goodreads.* https://www.goodreads.com/author/quotes/3462191.Mohammed_bin_Rashid_Al_Maktoum

Quotes by various authors. (n.d.). *BrainyQuote.* https://www.brainyquote.com/

Quotes by various authors. (n.d.). *Goodreads.* https://www.goodreads.com/quotes

Ryan, P. (2023, July 29). *What's next for the Dubai property market?* The National News: Weekend. https://

www.thenationalnews.com/weekend/2023/07/28/
whats-next-for-the-dubai-property-market/

The sky's the limit! Top real estate developers in Dubai. (2023, October). *Bayut.* https://www.bayut.com/mybayut/real-estate-developers-dubai/

TESTIMONIALS

'Jasmine knows the market. She is transparent and honest and looks after customer interest. I definitely suggest her for future references.'

—Alessio La Rosa
(Elysian Mansion Homeowner)

'We were looking for a new three-bedroom villa when we met Jasmine. She helped us to find very quickly what we wanted within our defined budget. The transaction was very easy and friendly. Jasmine is a real real estate professional in Dubai; I can strongly recommend her.'

—Grozdana Maric
(Tilal Al Ghaf Homeowner)

'Jasmine was absolutely fantastic from the very beginning of our search until after we had moved in. She went above and beyond at each stage, getting us in to view under difficult conditions; securing a property at a good price; helping with setting up POA; coming with us to sign and set up. Meeting us with the keys to welcome us in. Checking in on us to this day. She listened to what we were looking for, understood the brief fully, and guided us when nervous. We highly recommend Jasmine!'

—Charlotte Young
(Homeowner in Tilal Al Ghaf)

Read more testimonials on
https://www.dubairealtycheck.com/

GLOSSARY

MOUs (Memoranda of Understanding)/ Form F

MOUs are formal agreements between two or more parties, outlining the terms and details of an understanding, including each party's requirements and responsibilities. It is a legally binding contract, also known as Contract F. They signify the intention to move forward with a deal and can be used in real estate transactions to detail the preliminary agreement between a buyer and seller.

Bayut

Bayut is a leading real estate portal in the UAE that provides listings for buying, selling, and renting properties. It features residential and commercial properties, including apartments, villas, offices, and retail spaces, offering a comprehensive search tool for users to find their desired properties.

Snagging Company

A snagging company specializes in identifying and documenting any issues or defects in a property before the final handover to the owner. These companies conduct thorough inspections to ensure all aspects of the property meet the agreed standards and specifications.

Defect Liability Period (DLP)

The Defect Liability Period is a specified timeframe after the completion and handover of a property during which the developer or contractor is responsible for repairing any defects that arise. This period ensures any construction or material issues are addressed without cost to the property owner.

Dubai Land Department (DLD)

A government entity responsible for regulating and overseeing all real estate activities in Dubai, including property registration, legal compliance, and dispute resolution.

Dubizzle Account

Dubizzle (dubai.dubizzle.com) is a popular classifieds platform in the UAE, allowing users to buy, sell, or find a wide range of items and services within their community. It is widely used for property listings, job postings, and second-hand goods, providing a community-based marketplace.

Form A

Form A is the agreement form used in Dubai real estate transactions to outline the terms between the seller and the real estate agent. This form officially appoints the agent to market the property and manage the sale process on behalf of the seller.

Form B

The agreement form used between a buyer and a real estate agent, detailing the agent's responsibilities in finding and negotiating the purchase of a property on behalf of the buyer.

No Objection Certificate (NOC)

A No Objection Certificate (NOC) is an official document issued by a relevant authority or developer, confirming that they have no objections to the specific action being taken, such as the transfer of property ownership. NOCs are essential for property transactions in Dubai.

RERA Licence

A RERA Licence is issued by the Real Estate Regulatory Authority (RERA) in Dubai, certifying that a real estate agent or broker is authorized to operate in the emirate. This license ensures that the agent meets the professional standards set by RERA and is legally allowed to conduct real estate transactions.

Super Agents

Super Agents are highly experienced and top-performing real estate agents recognized on Property Finder for their exceptional service, extensive market knowledge, and superior client satisfaction. They often handle high-profile and complex property transactions and are trusted for their expertise and professionalism.

"To take risk and fail is not a failure. Real failure is to fear taking any risk."*

—HIS HIGHNESS SHEIKH MOHAMMED
 BIN RASHID AL MAKTOUM

---

* https://sheikhmohammed.ae/en-us/quotes

ABOUT THE AUTHOR

Jasmine is a COA-certified architect turned RERA-certified property advisor. She is a seasoned oracle of real estate with a track record that speaks volumes. Her insights are not just theoretical but battle-tested strategies that have navigated the trickiest deals. Join her in this journey of turning challenges into triumphs—a narrative every savvy investor craves.

Keep Jasmine's expertise by your side, the maestro of strategic investments in Dubai, specialising in Tilal Al Ghaf (a crystal lagoon community developed by Majid Al Futtaim). With an Instagram handle (ms.tilalalghaf) that's become synonymous with premium gains, she's here to help you with smooth transitions and how to gain profits in real estate investment while avoiding the common pitfalls.

Investors, sellers, first-time buyers and mortgage enthusiasts: Are you ready to get on board Jasmine's next real-estate adventure? Then look out for Book 2 for some enticing insights!

Connect with Me:
Instagram: @ms.tilalalghaf and @dubairealtycheck
YouTube: https://www.youtube.com/@Mstilalalghaf/featured
Website: **https://www.dubairealtycheck.com/**

@MS.TILALALGHAF

Notes